To Damascus

Medeba

Mishor

Dibon

Machaerus

Arnon Gorge

M O A B

...ha

Callirrhoe

En Gedi

Dead Sea

Kir Hareseth

Wilderness

Masada

Bab edh-Dhra

Lisan

En Boqeq

Numeira

Mezad Zohar

Kh. Uza

Mt. Sodom

Valley of Salt (Siddim)

Zoar

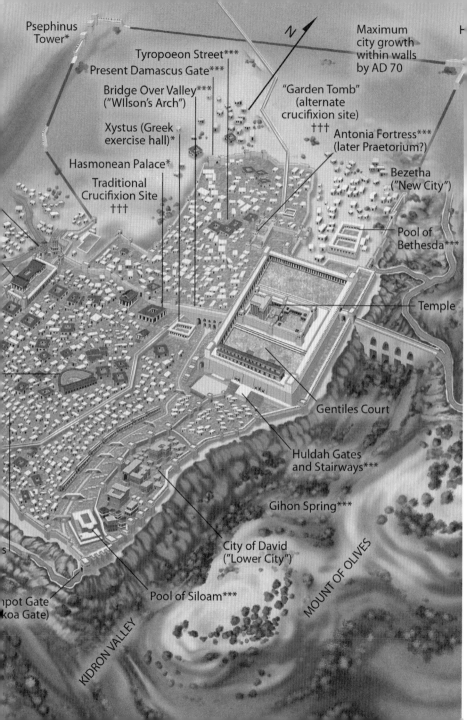

Psephinus Tower*

Tyropoeon Street***

Present Damascus Gate***

Bridge Over Valley***
("Wilson's Arch")

Xystus (Greek
exercise hall)*

Hasmonean Palace*

Traditional
Crucifixion Site
†††

Maximum
city growth
within walls
by AD 70

"Garden Tomb"
(alternate
crucifixion site)
†††

Antonia Fortress***
(later Praetorium?)

Bezetha
("New City")

Pool of
Bethesda***

Temple

Gentiles Court

Huldah Gates
and Stairways***

Gihon Spring***

City of David
("Lower City")

Pool of Siloam***

pot Gate
koa Gate)

KIDRON VALLEY

MOUNT OF OLIVES

In the
FOOTSTEPS
of the **SAVIOR**

ALSO BY MAX LUCADO

In the
FOOTSTEPS
of the SAVIOR

FOLLOWING JESUS THROUGH
THE HOLY LAND

MAX LUCADO

THOMAS NELSON
Since 1798

Portions of this book were adapted from: *A Gentle Thunder, A Love Worth Giving, And the Angels Were Silent, Begin Again, Fearless, Glory Days, God Came Near, Grace, Great Day Every Day, He Chose the Nails, He Still Moves Stones, Jesus, Just Like Jesus, The Applause of Heaven,* and *Unshakable Hope.*

Published in Nashville, Tennessee, by Thomas Nelson. Thomas Nelson is a registered trademark of HarperCollins Christian Publishing, Inc.

Scripture quotations are taken from the Holy Bible, New International Version®, NIV®. Copyright © 1973, 1978, 1984, 2011 by Biblica, Inc.® Used by permission of Zondervan. All rights reserved worldwide. www.zondervan.com.The "NIV" and "New International Version" are trademarks registered in the United States Patent and Trademark Office by Biblica, Inc.®

Other Scripture references are from the following sources: Scripture quotations marked AMPC are taken from the Amplified® Bible. Copyright © 1954, 1958, 1962, 1964,1965, 1987 by The Lockman Foundation. Used by permission. www.Lockman. org. Scripture quotations marked CEV are taken from the Contemporary English Version. Copyright © 1991, 1992, 1995 by American Bible Society. Used by permission. Scripture quotations marked ESV are taken from The Holy Bible, English Standard Version®. Copyright © 2001 by Crossway, a publishing ministry of Good News Publishers. Used by permission. All rights reserved. Scripture quotations marked GNT are taken from the Good News Translation in Today's English Version— Second Edition. Copyright © 1992 by American Bible Society. Used by permission. Scripture quotations marked JB are taken from *The Jerusalem Bible.* © 1966 by Darton Longman & Todd Ltd. and Doubleday and Company Ltd. Scripture quotations marked KJV are taken from the King James Version. Public domain. Scripture quotations marked THE MESSAGE are taken from *The Message.* Copyright © 1993, 2002, 2018 by Eugene H. Peterson. Used by permission of NavPress. All rights reserved. Represented by Tyndale House Publishers, a Division of Tyndale House Ministries. Scripture quotations marked NASB are taken from the New American Standard Bible® 1995 (NASB). Copyright © 1960, 1962, 1963, 1968, 1971, 1972, 1973, 1975, 1977, 1995 by The Lockman Foundation. Used by permission. www.Lockman.org. Scripture quotations marked NCV are taken from the New Century Version®. Copyright © 2005 by Thomas Nelson. Used by permission. All rights reserved. Scripture quotations marked NEB are taken from the New English Bible. Copyright © Cambridge University Press and Oxford University Press 1961, 1970. All rights reserved. Scripture quotations marked NKJV are taken from the New King James Version®. Copyright © 1982 by Thomas Nelson. Used by permission. All rights reserved. Scripture quotations marked NLT are taken from the Holy Bible, New Living Translation. Copyright © 1996, 2004, 2015 by Tyndale House Foundation. Used by permission of Tyndale House Ministries, Carol Stream, Illinois 60188. All rights reserved. Scripture quotations marked PHILLIPS are taken from The New Testament in Modern English by J. B. Phillips. Copyright © 1960, 1972 J. B. Phillips. Administered by The Archbishops' Council of the Church of England. Used by permission. Scripture quotations marked RSV are taken from the Revised Standard Version of the Bible. Copyright © 1946, 1952, and 1971 National Council of the Churches of Christ in the United States of America. Used by permission. All rights reserved. Scripture quotations marked TLB are taken from The Living Bible. Copyright © 1971. Used by permission of Tyndale House Publishers, a Division of Tyndale House Ministries, Carol Stream, Illinois 60188. All rights reserved.

Photography: Beth Rubin (B. Creative Inspiration, LLC); Cover Design: Jamie DeBruyn; Interior Design: Kristen Sasamoto

ISBN 978-1-4003-3518-3 (audiobook)   ISBN 978-1-4003-3516-9 (hardcover)
ISBN 978-1-4003-3517-6 (eBook)

Library of Congress Cataloging-in-Publication Data on File

Printed in the United States of America

23 24 25 26 27   LSC   6 5 4 3 2 1

Denalyn and I happily dedicate this book to Steve and Ruth Dick. Thanks to your skill, grace, and devotion, tens of thousands of people have walked the land where Jesus walked. May God bless you for being a blessing to Israel.

CONTENTS

CONTENTS

PART 3: THE CROSSROADS AND THE CROSS

ACKNOWLEDGMENTS

Steve Dick, president of Inspiration Cruises and Tours, for organizing the Israel tour upon which this project is based.

Samuel Smadja, of Sar-El Tours and Conferences, for his friendship and support in Israel, including coordinating the filming of the on-location teaching segments.

Mark Weising and Harper Christian Resources for creating a video study from footage shot by others halfway around the world. The teamwork of the body of Christ is beautiful to behold.

Beth Rubin, of B Creative Photography, for capturing the beauty of Israel in the images you see in this book.

The wonderful people of Israel. Thank you for opening your arms to those who love your land.

Steve and Cheryl Green, for tirelessly organizing the countless details of many journeys to the Holy Land.

Greg and Susan Ligon, for walking the land with us and suggesting this initiative.

ACKNOWLEDGMENTS

Angela Guzman, Janene MacIvor, and Karen Hill, who shepherded this project from infancy to publication.

Carol Bartley, Andrea Lucado Ramsay, Michael Briggs, and Tim Paulson. Your editorial savvy, skill, and oversight made this book possible.

INTRODUCTION

P ress me to select my favorite spot in Israel, and I will refuse. "It can't be done," I will tell you. "There are too many! The Garden Tomb. The Via Dolorosa. The Sea of Galilee. The Wailing Wall. How could a person select one over the others?"

Yet you insist. You want me to winnow the list down to one location. Finally I sigh and say, "Okay." I open a map of Israel and lead you and your imagination some twenty-nine miles north of the Sea of Galilee. The site is called Caesarea Philippi, named for Philip II, the third son of Herod the Great. It sits on the northern-most border of Israel, literally on the boundary between Israel and the world.

The location is stunning and dramatic. It boasts a cliff and, at its base, a cave. Visitors gaze up at the cliff and down into the yawning mouth of the grotto. Water springs from the ground beneath the cave, resulting in a flowing river of fresh water.

While the area is radiantly beautiful, its history is shadowy.

Caesarea Philippi has long been associated with idolatry. Fourteen temples dedicated to the worship of Baal have been identified in the vicinity. Herod the Great erected a temple in the front of the cave for worshiping Caesar Augustus. Neighboring temples were constructed for the worship of Zeus and other gods of the Greek and Roman cultures.

One god received more attention than any of the others—Pan, a Greek deity who was thought to have lived in the cave. Worship of Pan involved unspeakable sexual perversion.

It's no surprise, then, that an inscription designates the cave and the spring as the "Gate of Hell." Also, the chasm was deeper than any of the ancient peoples could plumb, so they assumed it was an entryway into the underworld, Hades or hell.

It was here, in this location, that Jesus asked his followers the watershed question: "Who do people say the Son of Man is?" (Matt. 16:13). The followers were quick to answer. Apparently they were privy to the word on the street. They listed the common assumptions: John the Baptist, Elijah, Jeremiah.

Jesus then asked for their opinion.

"But what about you? Who do you say I am?" (v. 15).

It is as if Jesus deliberately set himself, a humble woodworker, against the religions of the world, in all their splendor, in all their glory, and asked, "Who do you say that I am?"

On one occasion while touring Israel, a dozen or so of our tour group were standing together on the grounds. I asked if each of them would be willing to receive and then reply to the question of Jesus. They agreed. So I asked each person: "Who do you say that Jesus is?" And each person, in his or her own words, affirmed the confession made by Peter: "You are the Christ, the Son of the living God" (v. 16 NCV).

Jesus, upon hearing the words of Peter, declared, "On this rock I will build My church, and the gates of Hades shall not prevail against it" (v. 18 NKJV).

Can we imagine Jesus gesturing toward the cave as if defying the devil himself? *Hell itself will collapse. All this falsehood, all this immorality, all this deceit and death—it shall not withstand the assault of the church.*

Two thousand years later his pronouncement still stands. The proclamation that echoed in the cavern has reverberated through the ages.

What a promise and what a place to make it.

This is the wonder of the land where Jesus walked. Each square mile seems to have a message. I pray that the pages of this book bring those messages to life in your life. This weary world is in desperate need of a Savior. Thank God we have one. We can walk where he walked and ponder the promises he made. May you hear him as he speaks to you. May you be changed as you journey in the footsteps of the Savior.

PART 1

THE JOURNEY

Cathedral - Bethlehem

Bethlehem. Star-filled skies, bone-weary travelers, shepherds, and a new baby. Bethlehem reminds us of the most remarkable event in human history: the moment the Savior came to earth clothed in humility and humanity.

Today, centuries beyond that main event, a small chapel marks the probable birthplace of Jesus. Behind a high altar in the church lies a cavern lit by silver lamps. Enter the main edifice and admire the ancient church. Enter the quiet cave where a star embedded in the floor notes the birth of the King of heaven. There is one stipulation, however. You must bend down. The doorway is so low you can't enter standing up.

The same is true of Christ. You can see the world while standing tall, but to witness the Savior, you have to get on your knees.

CHAPTER 1

THE ARRIVAL

The noise and the bustle began earlier than usual in the village. As night gave way to dawn, people were already on the streets. Vendors were positioning themselves on the corners of the most heavily traveled avenues. Store owners were unlocking the doors to their shops. Children were awakened by the excited barking of the street dogs and the complaints of donkeys pulling carts.

The owner of the inn had awakened earlier than most in the town. After all, the inn was full, all the beds taken. Every available mat or blanket had been put to use. Soon all the customers would be stirring, and there would be a lot of work to do.

One's imagination is kindled thinking about the conversation of the innkeeper and his family at the breakfast table. Did anyone mention the arrival of the young couple the night before? Did anyone ask about their welfare? Did anyone comment on the pregnancy of the girl on the donkey? Perhaps someone raised the subject. But at best it was raised, not discussed. There was nothing novel about them. They were, possibly, one of several families turned away that night.

Besides, who had time to talk about one specific young couple when there was so much excitement in the air? Augustus did the economy of Bethlehem a favor when he decreed that a census should be taken. Who could remember when such commerce had hit the village?

No, it is doubtful that anyone mentioned the couple's arrival or wondered about the condition of the girl. They were too busy. The day was upon them. The day's bread had to be made. The morning's chores had to be done. There was too much to do to imagine that the impossible had occurred: God had entered the world as a baby.

Yet, were someone to chance upon the sheep stable on the outskirts of Bethlehem that morning, what a peculiar scene they would behold.

The stable stinks as all stables do. The stench of urine, dung, and sheep reeks pungently in the air. The ground is hard, the hay scarce. Cobwebs cling to the ceiling, and a mouse scurries across the dirt floor.

A more lowly place of birth could not exist.

Off to one side sits a group of shepherds. They sit silently on the floor, perhaps perplexed, perhaps in awe, no doubt in amazement. Their night watch had been interrupted by an explosion of light from heaven and a symphony of angels. God goes to those who have time to hear him, so on this cloudless night he went to simple shepherds.

Near the young mother stands the weary father. If anyone is dozing, he is. He can't remember the last time he sat down. And now that the excitement has subsided a bit, now that Mary and the baby are comfortable, he leans against the wall of the stable and feels his eyelids grow heavy. He still hasn't figured it all out. The mystery of the event puzzles him. But he hasn't the energy to wrestle with the questions now. What's important is that the baby is fine and Mary is safe. As sleep comes, he remembers the name the angel told him to use . . . *Jesus.* "We will call him Jesus."

Wide awake is Mary. My, how young she looks! Her head rests on the soft leather of Joseph's saddle. The pain has been eclipsed by wonder. She looks at the face of the baby. Her son. Her Lord. His Majesty. At this point in history the human being who best understands who God is and what he is doing is a teenage girl in a smelly stable. She can't take her eyes off him. Somehow Mary knows she is holding God. *So this is he.* She remembers the words of the angel. "His kingdom will never end."[1]

He looks like anything but a king. His face is prunish and red. His cry, though strong and healthy, is still the helpless and piercing cry of a baby. And he is absolutely dependent upon Mary for his well-being.

Majesty in the midst of the mundane. Holiness in the filth of sheep manure and sweat. Divinity entering the world on the floor of a stable, through the womb of a teenager, and in the presence of a carpenter.

She touches the face of the infant-God. *How long was your journey!*

This baby had overlooked the universe. These rags keeping

him warm were the robes of eternity. His golden throne room had been abandoned in favor of a dirty sheep pen. And worshiping angels had been replaced by kind but bewildered shepherds.

Meanwhile the city hums. The merchants are unaware that God has visited their planet. The innkeeper would never believe that he had just sent God into the cold. And the people would scoff at anyone who told them the Messiah lay in the arms of a teenager on the outskirts of their village. They were all too busy to consider the possibility.

Those who missed His Majesty's arrival that night missed it not because of evil acts or malice; no, they missed it because they simply weren't looking.

Little has changed in the last two thousand years, has it?

THE TEMPLE VISIT

Life is tough enough as it is. It gets even tougher when we're headed in the wrong direction.

One of the incredible abilities of Jesus was to stay on target. His life never got off track. He had no money, no computers, no jets, no administrative assistants or staff, yet Jesus did what many of us fail to do. He kept his life on course.

As the young Jesus looked across the horizon of his future, he could see many targets. Many flags were flapping in the wind, each of which he could have pursued. He could have been a political revolutionary. He could have been a national leader. He could have been content to be a teacher and educate minds or to be a physician and heal bodies. But in the end he chose to be a Savior and save souls.

Anyone near Christ for any length of time heard it from Jesus himself. "The Son of Man came to find lost people and save them" (Luke 19:10 NCV). "The Son of Man did not come to be served. He came to serve others and to give his life as a ransom for many people" (Mark 10:45 NCV).

The heart of Christ was relentlessly focused on one task. The day he left the carpentry shop in Nazareth he had one ultimate aim—the cross of Calvary. He was so focused that his final words were "It is finished" (John 19:30 NCV).

How could Jesus say he was finished? There were still the hungry to feed, the sick to heal, the untaught to instruct, and the unloved to love. How could he say he was finished? Simple. He had completed his designated task. His commission was fulfilled. The painter could set aside his brush, the sculptor lay down his chisel, the writer put away his pen. The job was done.

Wouldn't you love to be able to say the same? Wouldn't you love to look back on your life and know you had done what you were called to do?

DISTRACTED HEARTS

Our lives tend to be so scattered. Intrigued by one trend only until the next comes along. Suckers for the latest craze or quick fix. This project, then another. Lives with no strategy, no goal, no defining priority. Playing the holes out of order. Erratic. Hesitant.

Living life with the hiccups. We are easily distracted by the small things and forget the big things.

How do we keep from being distracted by the small things in life? God wants us to be just like Jesus and have focused hearts. How do we stay on target? By answering the following four simple questions, we can be more like Jesus; we can stay on course with our lives. *Am I fitting into God's plan? What are my longings? What are my abilities? Am I serving God now?*

AM I FITTING INTO GOD'S PLAN?

Romans 8:28 says, "We know that all that happens to us is working for our good if we love God and are fitting into his plans" (TLB). The first step for focusing your heart is to ask this question: Am I fitting into God's plan?

God's plan is to save his children. "He does not want anyone to be destroyed, but wants all to turn away from their sins" (2 Peter 3:9 GNT).

If God's goal is the salvation of the world, then my goal should be the same. The details will differ from person to person, but the big picture is identical for all of us. "We're Christ's representatives. God uses us to persuade men and women" (2 Cor. 5:20 THE MESSAGE). Regardless of what you don't know about your future, one thing is certain: you are intended to contribute to the good plan of God, to tell others about the God who loves them and longs to bring them home.

But exactly how are you to contribute? What is your specific assignment? Let's seek the answer with a second question.

WHAT ARE MY LONGINGS?

This question may surprise you. Perhaps you thought your longings had nothing to do with keeping your life on track. I couldn't disagree more. Your heart is crucial. Psalm 37:4 says, "Enjoy serving the LORD, and he will give you what you want" (NCV). When we submit to God's plans, we can trust our desires. Our assignment is found at the intersection of God's plan and our pleasures. What do you love to do? What brings you joy? What gives you a sense of satisfaction?

Some long to feed the poor. Others enjoy leading the church. Others relish singing or teaching or holding the hands of the sick or counseling the confused. Each of us has been made to serve God in a unique way.

> We are God's handiwork, created in Christ Jesus to do good works, which God prepared in advance for us to do. (Eph. 2:10).
>
> You made all the delicate, inner parts of my body and knit them together in my mother's womb. . . . Your workmanship is marvelous. . . . You were there while I was being formed. . . . You saw me before I was born and scheduled each day of my life before I began to breathe. (Ps. 139:13–16 TLB)

You are a custom design; you are tailor-made. God prescribed your birth. Regardless of the circumstances that surrounded your arrival, you are not an accident. God planned you before you were born.

The longings of your heart, then, are not incidental; they are critical messages. The desires of your heart are not to be ignored; they are to be consulted. As the wind turns the weather vane, so God uses your passions to turn your life. God is too gracious to ask you to do something you hate.

Be careful, however. Don't consider your desires without considering your skills. Move quickly to the third question.

WHAT ARE MY ABILITIES?

There are some things we want to do but simply aren't equipped to accomplish. I, for example, have the desire to sing. Singing for others would give me wonderful satisfaction. The problem is, it wouldn't give the same satisfaction to my audience. I am what you might call a prison singer—I never have the key, and I'm always behind a few bars.

Paul gives good advice in Romans 12:3: "Have a sane estimate of your capabilities" (PHILLIPS).

In other words, be aware of your strengths. When you teach, do people listen? When you lead, do people follow? When you administer, do things improve? Where are you most productive? Identify your strengths, and then—this is important—major in them. Take a few irons out of the fire so this one can get hot. Failing to focus on our strengths may prevent us from accomplishing the unique tasks God has called us to do.

We cannot meet every need in the world. We cannot please every person in the world. We cannot satisfy every request in the world. But some of us try. And in the end we run out of fuel. Have a sane estimate of your abilities and stick to them.

One final question is needed.

AM I SERVING GOD NOW?

Upon reading this you may start feeling restless. *Maybe I need to change jobs. Perhaps I should relocate. I guess Max is telling me I need to go to seminary . . .* No, not necessarily.

Again, Jesus is the ideal example. When do we get our first clue that he knows he is the Son of God? In the temple of Jerusalem. He is twelve years old. His parents are three days into the return trip to Nazareth before they notice he is missing. They find him in the temple studying with the leaders. When they ask him for an explanation, he says, "Did you not know that I must be about My Father's business?" (Luke 2:49 NKJV).

As a young boy, Jesus already senses the call of God. But what does he do next? Recruit apostles and preach sermons and perform miracles? No, he goes home to his folks and learns the family business.

That is exactly what you should do. Want to bring focus to your life? Do what Jesus did. Go home, love your family, and take care of business. *But, Max, I want to be a missionary.* Your first mission field is under your roof. What makes you think they'll believe you overseas if they don't believe you across the hall?

But, Max, I'm ready to do great things for God. Good, do them at work. Be a good employee. Show up on time with a good attitude. Don't complain or grumble, but "work as if you were doing it for the Lord, not for people" (Col. 3:23 NCV).

Pretty simple plan, don't you think? It's even easy to remember. Perhaps you caught the acrostic:

Am I fitting into God's **P**lan?

What are my **L**ongings?

What are my **A**bilities?

Am I serving God **N**ow?

Why don't you take a few moments and evaluate your direction. Ask yourself the four questions. You may find that you need to follow Jesus' example more closely.

God allows you to start fresh at any point in life. "From now on, then, you must live the rest of your earthly lives controlled by God's will and not by human desires" (1 Peter 4:2 GNT).

Circle the words *from now on*. God will give you a fresh scorecard. Regardless of what has controlled you in the past, it's never too late to get your life on course and be a part of God's plan.

QUESTIONS FOR REFLECTION

1. This chapter opens with a bustling scene in the town of Bethlehem.
   - What was Bethlehem like?
   - What was happening in the city the day Jesus was born?
   - Why did Mary and Joseph's arrival in Bethlehem and Jesus' birth go unnoticed?

2. Max points out that not much has changed—we are still too distracted to stop and notice Christ in our midst. Our world offers a lot of distractions: social media, endless Netflix series, online shopping, and texting, to name a few.

- What diverts your attention most throughout the day?
- Which of these distractions keep you from noticing Jesus' presence in your life?
- What helps you notice Jesus' presence in your life?

3. Read Mark 10:45 and Luke 19:10. According to these verses, what was Jesus' mission on earth?
   - How did he achieve this mission?
   - Do you believe you have a mission or purpose in life? If so, what is it? If not, why not?
   - Jesus' mission was accomplished. We know this because he said, "It is finished" right before his death on the cross. What do you hope to finish or achieve in your life?
   - What is distracting you from this purpose?

4. Max lists four questions that can help guide you in becoming more like Christ and staying on course. Reflect on those questions below.
   - Am I fitting into God's plan? (2 Peter 3:9)
   - What are your longings, the desires of your heart? This question may be difficult to answer. Consider why that is before attempting to answer it. Acknowledge any tension you feel.
   - What are my unique strengths and abilities? As above, if this question is difficult to answer, pause and

consider why. Or ask someone who knows you well to help you.

- How did Jesus serve God before his public ministry began? (Luke 2:51–52) How could I serve God where I am today with the people around me?

CHAPTER 2

LIVING IN A CARPENTER'S FAMILY

The white space between Bible verses is fertile soil for questions. One can hardly read Scripture without whispering, "I wonder . . ."

"I wonder if Eve ever ate any more fruit."

"I wonder if Noah slept well during storms."

"I wonder if Jonah liked fish or if Jeremiah had friends."

"Did Moses avoid bushes? Did Jesus tell jokes? Did Peter ever try water-walking again?"

"Would any woman have married Paul had he asked?"

The Bible is a fence full of knotholes through which we can peek but not see the whole picture. It's a scrapbook of snapshots capturing people in encounters with God but not always recording the result. So we wonder:

When the woman caught in adultery went home, what did she say to her husband?

After the demoniac was delivered, what did he do for a living?

After Jairus's daughter was raised from the dead, did she ever regret it?

Knotholes and snapshots and lots of "I wonder . . ." You'll find them in every chapter about every person. But nothing stirs as many questions as does the birth of Christ. Characters appear and disappear before we can ask them anything. The innkeeper too busy to welcome God—did he ever learn who he turned away? The shepherds—did they ever hum the song the angels sang? The wise men who followed the star—what was it like to worship a toddler? And Joseph, especially Joseph. I've got questions for Joseph.

Did you ever look up from your prayers and see Jesus listening?

Whatever happened to the wise men?

Whatever happened to you?

We don't know what happened to Joseph. His role in Act I is so crucial that we expect to see him in the rest of the drama. But with the exception of a short scene with twelve-year-old Jesus in Jerusalem, he never reappears. The rest of his life is left to speculation, and we are left with our questions.

But of all my questions, my first would be about Bethlehem. I'd like to know about the night in the stable. I can picture Joseph there. Moonlit pastures. Stars twinkle above. Bethlehem sparkles in the distance. There he is, pacing outside the stable.

What was he thinking while Jesus was being born? What was on his mind while Mary was giving birth? He'd done all he could do—heated the water and prepared a place for Mary to lie down. He'd made Mary as comfortable as she could be in a barn, and then he stepped out. She'd asked to be alone, and Joseph had never felt more so.

In that eternity between his wife's dismissal and Jesus' arrival, what was he thinking? He walked into the night and looked at the stars. Did he pray?

For some reason I don't see him silent; I see Joseph animated, pacing. Head shaking one minute, fist shaking the next. This isn't what he had in mind. I wonder what he said . . .

This isn't the way I planned it, God. Not at all. My child being born in a stable? This isn't the way I thought it would be. A cave with sheep and donkeys, hay and straw? My wife giving birth with only the stars to hear her pain?

This isn't at all what I imagined. No, I imagined family. I imagined grandmothers. I imagined neighbors clustered outside the door and friends standing at my side. I imagined the house erupting with the first cry of the infant. Slaps on the back. Loud laughter. Jubilation.

That's how I thought it would be.

The midwife would hand me my child, and all the people would applaud. Mary would rest, and we would celebrate. All of Nazareth would celebrate.

But now. Now look. Nazareth is a five-day journey away. And here we are in a . . . in a sheep pasture. Who will celebrate with us? The sheep? The shepherds? The stars?

Did I miss something? Did I, God?

When you sent the angel and spoke of the son being born, this isn't what I pictured. I envisioned Jerusalem, the temple, the priests, and the people gathered to watch. A pageant perhaps. A parade. A banquet at least. I mean, this is the Messiah!

Or, if not born in Jerusalem, how about Nazareth? This is not the way I wanted it to be! This is not the way I wanted my son—

Oh my, I did it again. I did it again, didn't I, Father? I don't mean to do that; it's just that I forget. He's not my son . . . he's yours.

The child is yours. The plan is yours. The idea is yours. And forgive me for asking, but . . . is this how God enters the world? The coming of the angel, I've accepted. The questions people asked about the pregnancy, I can tolerate. The trip to Bethlehem, fine. But why a birth in a stable, God?

Any minute now Mary will give birth. Not to a child, but to the Messiah. Not to an infant, but to God. That's what the angel said. That's what Mary believes. And, God, my God, that's what I want to believe. But surely you can understand; it's not easy. It seems so . . . so . . . so . . . bizarre.

I'm unaccustomed to such strangeness, God. I'm a carpenter. I make things fit. I square off the edges. I follow the plumb line. I measure twice before I cut once. Surprises are not the friend of a builder. I like to know the plan. I like to see the plan before I begin.

But this time I'm not the builder, am I? This time I'm a tool. A hammer in your grip. A nail between your fingers. A chisel in your hands. This project is yours, not mine.

I guess it's foolish of me to question you. Forgive my struggling. Trust doesn't come easy to me, God. But you never said it would be easy, did you?

One final thing, Father. The angel you sent? Any chance you could send another? If not an angel, maybe a person? I don't know anyone around here, and some company would be nice. Maybe the innkeeper or a traveler? Even a shepherd would do.

I wonder. Did Joseph ever pray such a prayer? Perhaps he did. Perhaps he didn't.

But you probably have.

You've stood where Joseph stood. Caught between what God says and what makes sense to you. You've done what he told you to do only to wonder if it was God speaking in the first place. You've stared into a sky blackened with doubt. And you've asked what Joseph asked.

You've asked if you're still on the right road. You've asked if you were supposed to turn left when you turned right. And you've asked if there is a plan behind this scheme. Things haven't turned out like you thought they would.

Each of us knows what it's like to search the night for light. Not outside a stable, but perhaps outside an emergency room. Or on the gravel of a roadside. Or on the manicured grass of a cemetery. We've asked our questions. We've questioned God's plan. And we've wondered why God does what he does.

The Bethlehem sky is not the first to hear the pleadings of a confused pilgrim.

If you are asking what Joseph asked, let me urge you to do what Joseph did. Obey. That's what he did. He obeyed. He obeyed when the angel called. He obeyed when Mary explained.

He obeyed when God sent them to Bethlehem and Egypt.

He was obedient to God.

He was obedient when the sky was bright.

He was obedient when the sky was dark.

He didn't let his confusion disrupt his obedience. He didn't know everything. But he did what he knew to do. He shut down his business, packed up his family, and went to another country. Why? Because that's what God said to do.

What about you? Just like Joseph, you can't see the whole picture. Just like Joseph, your task is to see that Jesus is brought into your part of your world. And just like Joseph, you have a choice: to obey or disobey. Because Joseph obeyed, God used him to change the world.

Can he do the same with you?

God still looks for Josephs today. Men and women who believe that God is not through with this world. Common people who serve an uncommon God.

Will you be that kind of person? Will you serve . . . even when you don't understand?

No, the Bethlehem sky was not the first to hear the pleadings of an honest heart, nor the last. And perhaps God didn't answer every question for Joseph. But he answered the most important one. "Are you still with me, God?" And through the first cries of the God-child, the answer came.

"Yes. Yes, Joseph. I'm with you."

There are many questions about the Bible that we won't be able to answer until we get home. Many knotholes and snapshots. Many times we will muse, "I wonder . . ."

But in our wonderings there is one question we never need to ask: Does God care? Do we matter to God? Does he still love his children?

Through the small face of the stable-born baby, he says yes.

Yes, your sins are forgiven.

Yes, your name is written in heaven.

Yes, death has been defeated.

And, yes, God has entered your world.

Immanuel. God is with us.

DEALING WITH DIFFICULTIES

It may surprise you to know that Jesus had a difficult family. It may surprise you to know that Jesus had a family at all! You may not be aware that Jesus had brothers and sisters. He did. Quoting Jesus' hometown critics, Mark wrote, "[Jesus] is just the carpenter, the son of Mary and the brother of James, Joseph, Judas, and Simon. And his sisters are here with us" (Mark 6:3 NCV).

And it may surprise you to know that his family was less than perfect. They were. If your family doesn't appreciate you, take heart. Neither did Jesus'. "A prophet is honored everywhere except in his hometown and with his own people and in his own home" (Mark 6:4 NCV).

I wonder what he meant when he said those last five words. He went to the synagogue where he was asked to speak. The people were proud that this hometown boy had done well—until they heard what he said. He referred to himself as the Messiah, the one to fulfill prophecy.

Their response? "Isn't this Joseph's son?" Translation? This is no Messiah! He's just like us! God doesn't speak through familiar people.

One minute he was a hero, the next a heretic. Look what happened next. "They got up, forced Jesus out of town, and took him to the edge of the cliff on which the town was built. They planned to throw him off the edge, but Jesus walked through the crowd and went on his way" (Luke 4:29–30 NCV).

What an ugly moment! Jesus' neighborhood friends tried to kill him. But even uglier than what we see is what we don't see. Notice what is missing from this verse. Note what words should be there but aren't: "They planned to throw him over the cliff, but Jesus' brothers came and stood up for him."

We'd like to read that, but we can't, because it doesn't say that. That's not what happened. When Jesus was in trouble, his brothers were invisible.

They weren't always invisible, however. There was a time when they spoke. There was a time when they were seen with him in public. Not because they were proud of him but because they were ashamed of him. "His family . . . went to get him because they thought he was out of his mind" (Mark 3:21 NCV).

Jesus' siblings thought their brother was a lunatic. They weren't proud—they were embarrassed!

So Jesus' brothers said to him, "You should leave here and go to Judea so your followers there can see the miracles you do. Anyone who wants to be well known does not hide what he does. If you are doing these things, show yourself to the world." (John 7:3–4 NCV)

Listen to the sarcasm in those words! How did Jesus put up with this ridicule?

Jesus gives us some answers.

It's worth noting that he didn't try to control his family's behavior, nor did he let their behavior control his. He didn't demand that they agree with him. He didn't sulk when they insulted him. He didn't make it his mission to try to please them.

Each of us has a fantasy that our family will be picture perfect, an expectation that our dearest friends will be our next of kin. Jesus didn't have that expectation. Look how he defined his family: "My true brother and sister and mother are those who do what God wants" (Mark 3:35 NCV).

When Jesus' brothers didn't share his convictions, he didn't try to force them. He recognized that his spiritual family could provide what his physical family didn't. If Jesus himself couldn't force his family to share his convictions, what makes you think you can force yours?

We can't control the way our families respond to us. When it comes to the behavior of others toward us, our hands are tied. We have to move beyond the naive expectation that if we do good, people will treat us right. The fact is they may or they may not—we cannot control how people respond to us.

As long as you think you can control people's behavior toward you, you are held in bondage by their opinions. If you think you can control their opinion and their opinion isn't positive, then guess whom you have to blame? Yourself.

It's a game with unfair rules and fatal finishes. Jesus didn't play it, nor should you.

We don't know if Joseph affirmed his son Jesus in his ministry—but we know God did: "This is my Son, whom I love, and I am very pleased with him" (Matt. 3:17 NCV).

I can't assure you that your family will ever give you the blessing you seek, but I know God will. Let God give you what your family doesn't. If your earthly father doesn't affirm you, then let your heavenly Father take his place.

How do you do that? By emotionally accepting God as your Father. You see, it's one thing to accept him as Lord, another to recognize him as Savior—but it's another matter entirely to accept him as Father.

To recognize God as Lord is to acknowledge that he is sovereign and supreme in the universe. To accept him as Savior is to accept his gift of salvation offered on the cross. To regard him as Father is to go a step further. Ideally, a father is the one in your life who provides and protects. That is exactly what God has done.

He has provided for your needs (Matt. 6:25–34). He has protected you from harm (Ps. 139:5). He has adopted you (Eph. 1:5). And he has given you his name (1 John 3:1).

God has proven himself as a faithful father. Now it falls to us to be trusting children. Let God give you what your family doesn't. Let him fill the void others have left. Rely upon him for your affirmation and encouragement. Look at Paul's words: "You are God's child, and God will give you the blessing he promised, because *you are his child*" (Gal. 4:7 NCV, emphasis added).

Having your family's approval is desirable but not necessary for happiness and not always possible. Jesus did not let the difficult dynamic of his family overshadow his call from God.

What happened to Jesus' family?

Mine with me a golden nugget hidden in a vein of the book of Acts. "Then [the disciples] went back to Jerusalem from the Mount of Olives. . . . They all continued praying together with some women, including Mary the mother of Jesus, and Jesus' brothers" (Acts 1:12, 14 NCV).

What a change! The ones who had mocked him now worship him. The ones who had pitied him now pray for him. What if Jesus had disowned them? Or worse still, what if he'd suffocated his family with his demand for change?

He didn't. He instead gave them space, time, and grace. And because he did, they changed. How much did they change?

One brother became an apostle (Gal. 1:19), and others became missionaries (1 Cor. 9:5).

So don't lose heart. God still changes families. A difficult family member today might be your dearest friend tomorrow.

QUESTIONS FOR REFLECTION

1. Joseph wasn't expecting his son to be born away from home in Bethlehem, in a cave filled with animals, and placed in a trough as a makeshift bed. He was "caught between what God says and what makes sense" in human terms (p. 19).

- What circumstance in your life has you standing where Joseph stood—caught between what you believe God told you and what makes sense to you?
- What did Joseph do in the midst of his doubt and uncertainty?
- What would it look like for you to do the same?

2. Jesus was born in Bethlehem in Judea, but he grew up in Nazareth, farther north in the region of Galilee. Even though Nazareth was home, that didn't mean his family and neighbors supported his ministry. Read Mark 3:20–21.
   - How did Jesus' family feel about his ministry?
   - Think about a time your family didn't support you or didn't understand something you felt passionate about or believed in.
   - How did this questioning or lack of support make you feel?

3. Jesus returned to Nazareth to preach during his ministry. Read in Luke 4:28–30 how his community responded to his sermon.
   - The mob likely took Jesus to a place called Mount Precipice, which looks over the city of Nazareth. Imagine Jesus looking down at his home, on the streets where he played as a child. Have you ever felt rejected by a community you were a part of? How did that rejection affect you?

- How does it feel to know that Jesus also was rejected by both his family and his community?

4. Max explained there are differences in accepting God as your Lord, accepting God as your Savior, and accepting God as your Father. What are those differences?
   - Do you believe you've accepted God as your Father? Why or why not?
   - Fill in the blanks: "Ideally, a father is the one in your life who ___ and ____" (p. 24).
   - Has your earthly father done this for you? If so, how? If not, how has that affected your relationship with him? Has it affected your view of God? If so, in what way?
   - What would it look like to let God fill any voids left by your family, whether that's your father, mother, or siblings?

CHAPTER 3

LEAVING HOME

Questions I'd like to ask Joseph:

What was it like watching Jesus pray?

How did he respond when he saw other kids giggling during the service at the synagogue?

When he saw a rainbow, did he ever mention a flood?

Did you ever feel awkward teaching him how he created the world?

When he saw a lamb being led to the slaughter, did he act differently?

Did you ever see him with a distant look on his face as if he were listening to someone you couldn't hear?

How did he act at funerals?

Did the thought ever occur to you that the God to whom you pray was asleep under your own roof?

Did you ever try to count the stars with him . . . and succeed?

Did he ever come home with a black eye?

How did he act when he got his first haircut?

Did he have any friends by the name of Judas?

Did he do well in school?

Did you ever scold him?

Did he ever have to ask a question about Scripture?

What do you think he thought when he saw a prostitute offering to the highest bidder the body he made?

Did he ever get angry when someone was dishonest with him?

Did you ever catch him pensively looking at the flesh on his arm while holding a clod of dirt?

Did he ever wake up afraid?

Who was his best friend?

When someone referred to Satan, how did he act?

Did you ever accidentally call him Father?

What did he and his cousin John talk about as kids?

Did his brothers and sisters understand what was happening?

Did you ever think, *That's God eating my soup*?

VICTORY OVER EVIL

I have a confession. I don't always finish what I start. Chances are I'm not alone. Any unfinished projects under your roof? Perhaps an exercise machine with the primary function thus far of holding towels? Or an unopened do-it-yourself pottery course? How about a half-finished patio deck or a half-planted garden? And let's not even touch the topic of diets and weight loss, okay?

You know as well as I do that it's one thing to start something. It's something else entirely to complete it. You may think I'm going to talk to you about the importance of finishing everything. Could be you are bracing yourself for a bit of chastising.

If so, relax. "Don't start what you can't finish" is not one of my points. And I'm not going to say anything about what is used to pave the road to hell. To be honest, I don't believe you should finish everything you start. There are certain quests better left undone, some projects wisely abandoned.

We can become so obsessed with completion that we become blind to effectiveness. Just because a project is on the table, it doesn't mean it can't be returned to the shelf. No, my desire is not to convince you to finish everything. My desire is to encourage you to finish the right thing. Certain races are optional—like washboard abs and speed-reading. Other races are essential—like the race of faith. Consider this admonition from the author of Hebrews: "Let us run the race that is before us and never give up" (12:1 NCV).

THE RACE

The word *race* is from the Greek word *agon*, from which we get the word *agony*. The Christian's race is not a jog but rather a demanding and grueling, sometimes agonizing race. It takes a massive effort to finish strong.

Likely you've noticed that many don't. Surely you've observed there are many on the side of the trail. They used to be running. There was a time when they kept the pace. But then weariness set in. They didn't think the run would be this tough. Or they were discouraged by a bump and daunted by a fellow runner. Whatever the reason, they don't run anymore. They may be Christians. They may come to church, but their hearts aren't in the race. They retired before their time. Unless something changes, their best work will have been their first work, and they will finish with a whimper.

By contrast Jesus' best work was his final work, and his strongest step was his last step. Our Master is the classic example of one who endured. The writer of Hebrews goes on to say that Jesus "held on while wicked people were doing evil things to him" (12:3 NCV). The Bible says Jesus "held on," implying that Jesus could have let go. He could have quit the race. But he didn't. He "held on while wicked people were doing evil things to him."

THE RESISTANCE

Have you ever thought about the evil things done to Christ? Can you think of times when Jesus could have given up? How about his time of temptation? You and I know what it is like to endure a moment of temptation or an hour of temptation, even a day of temptation. But forty days? That is what Jesus faced. "The Spirit led Jesus into the desert where the devil tempted Jesus for forty days" (Luke 4:1–2 NCV).

We imagine the wilderness temptation as three isolated events scattered over a forty-day period. Would that it had been. In reality Jesus' time of testing was nonstop; "the devil tempted Jesus for forty days." Satan got on Jesus like a shirt and refused to leave.

Every step, whispering in his ear. Every turn of the path, sowing doubt. Was Jesus impacted by the devil? Apparently so. Luke doesn't say that Satan tried to tempt Jesus. The verse doesn't read that the devil attempted to tempt Jesus. No the passage is clear: "the devil tempted Jesus." Jesus was tempted; he was tested. Tempted to change sides? Tempted to go home? Tempted to settle for a kingdom on earth? I don't know, but I know he was tempted. A war raged within. Stress stormed without. And since he was tempted, he could have quit the race. But he didn't. He kept on running.

Temptation didn't stop him, nor did accusations. Can you imagine what it would be like to run in a race and be criticized by the bystanders?

What if, in the toughest steps of the race, you heard words of accusation and not encouragement? And what if the accusations came from your neighbors and family?

How would you like somebody to yell these words at you as you ran:

"Hey, liar! Why don't you do something honest with your life?" (John 7:12)

"Here comes the foreigner. Why don't you go home where you belong?" (John 8:48)

"Since when do they let children of the devil enter the race?" (John 8:48)

That's what happened to Jesus. His own family called him a lunatic. His neighbors treated him even worse. When Jesus returned to his hometown, they tried to throw him off a cliff (Luke 4:29). But Jesus didn't quit running. Temptations didn't deter him. Accusations didn't defeat him. Nor did shame dishearten him.

I invite you to think carefully about the supreme test Jesus faced in the race. Hebrews 12:2 offers this intriguing statement: "[Jesus] accepted the shame as if it were nothing" (NCV).

Shame is a feeling of disgrace, embarrassment, humiliation. Forgive me for stirring the memory, but don't you have a shameful moment in your history? Can you imagine the horror you would feel if everyone knew about it? What if a video of that event were played before your family and friends? How would you feel?

That is exactly what Jesus felt. "Why?" you ask. He never did anything worthy of shame. No, but we did. And since on the cross God made him become sin (2 Cor. 5:21), Jesus was covered with shame. He was shamed before his family. Stripped naked before his own mother and loved ones. Shamed before his fellow men. Forced to carry a cross until the weight caused him to stumble. Shamed before his church. The pastors and elders of his day mocked him, calling him names. Shamed before the city of Jerusalem. Condemned to die a criminal's death. Parents likely pointed to him from a distance and told their children, "That's what they do to evil men."

But the shame before men didn't compare with the shame Jesus felt before his Father. Our individual shame seems too much to bear. Can you imagine bearing the collective shame of all humanity? One wave of shame after another was dumped on Jesus. Though he never cheated, he was convicted as a cheat. Though he never stole, heaven regarded him as a thief. Though he never lied, he was considered a liar. Though he never lusted, he bore the shame of an adulterer. Though he always believed, he endured the disgrace of an infidel.

Such words stir one urgent question: *How?* How did he endure such disgrace? What gave Jesus the strength to endure the shame of all the world? We need an answer, don't we? Like Jesus we are tempted. Like Jesus we are accused. Like Jesus we are ashamed. But unlike Jesus we give up. We give out. We sit down. How can we keep running as Jesus did? How can our hearts have the endurance Jesus had?

By focusing where Jesus focused: on "the joy that God put before him" (Heb. 12:2 NCV).

THE REWARD

This verse may very well be the greatest testimony ever written about the glory of heaven. Nothing is said about golden streets or angels' wings. No reference is made to music or feasts. Even the word *heaven* is missing from the verse. But though the word is missing, the power is not.

Remember, heaven was not foreign to Jesus. He is the only person to live on earth after he had lived in heaven. As believers, you and I will live in heaven after time on earth, but Jesus did just the opposite. He knew heaven before he came to earth. He knew what awaited him upon his return. And knowing what awaited him in heaven enabled him to bear the shame on earth.

"He accepted the shame as if it were nothing because of the joy that God put before him" (Heb. 12:2 NCV). In his final moments on earth, Jesus focused on the joy God put before him. He focused on the prize of heaven. By focusing on the prize, he was able not only to finish the race but to finish it strong.

I understand where Jesus found his strength. He lifted his eyes beyond the horizon and saw the table. He focused on the feast. And what he saw gave him strength to finish—and finish strong.

Such a moment awaits us. In a world oblivious to many things, we'll take our place at the table. In an hour that has no end, we will rest. Surrounded by saints and engulfed by Jesus himself, the work will, indeed, be finished. The final harvest will have been gathered, we will be seated, and Christ will christen the meal with these words: "Well done, good and faithful servant" (Matt. 25:23 KJV).

And in that moment, the race will have been worth it.

QUESTIONS FOR REFLECTION

1. Mary knew her son was both human and divine. Do you think Mary raised Jesus differently than her other children or the same? Why?
   - What do you think it was like for Jesus growing up in a normal village, Nazareth, with a normal family, knowing what God's ultimate plan for him was?
   - Do you tend to think of Jesus as fully human, or do you more often picture him as a divine being? Why do you think this is? Why were both essential for him?

2. Read Hebrews 12:1–2. What is the race that has been set out for us? How do we stay focused on this journey?

3. Even Jesus was tempted to stray from finishing the race. After being baptized in the Jordan River, Jesus was led into the Judean Desert to be tested. Read Luke 4:1–13.

  • How did Satan tempt Jesus?

  • How did Jesus respond to each temptation?

  • What are some of your greatest temptations, ones that get in the way of the race you're trying to finish?

  • What is a temptation that has reoccurred in your life? What has given you strength to overcome it?

  • Have you ever considered sharing a personal victory over temptation with someone else who is struggling? If so, how did that person receive your story?

4. Jesus finished his race on a cross on a large, skull-shaped rock called Golgotha outside of Jerusalem's gates. (*Golgotha* is an Aramaic word that means "skull.") While he hung there, he took on the sin and shame of man. The New Century Version translation of Hebrews 12:2 says, "[Jesus] accepted the shame as if it were nothing."

  • What does shame feel like for you?

  • Describe a time you felt shame.

  • Why is it important that Jesus felt shame just as you have felt it?

  • Has shame held you back in some way from this long journey of faith? If so, how can you overcome it?

5. According to Hebrews 12:2, why did Jesus endure this shame on the cross?

- Do you experience joy in Christ? If so, describe the experience.
- How could this joyful moment encourage you on your race today?
- How does the joy that has been set before all of us—being united with the Father in heaven—encourage you in your faith journey?

n Sea

re

**UPPER
GALILEE**

Mt. Meron

Kedesh

Hazor

Capernaum
Heptapegon
Taricheae
(Dalmanutha)
(Magadan)
(Magdala)
Kinnereth

Arbel Pass

Tiberias

**EASTERN
LOWER
GALILEE**

Hammath

Kedesh

Jabneel

Dan

Caesarea P

Korazin

Bethsaida
(Julias)?

Jordan R.

Gam

Bethsaida (Galilee)

*Plain of
Bethsaida*

*Plain of
Gennesaret*

*Sea of
Galilee*

Gergesa (Kursi)

Hippus

Beth Yerah

N. Jabneel

*Rift
Valley*

Hammath

Gadara

Yarmuk R.

Jordan R.

He

PART 2
THE MINISTRY

Sea of Galilee - Capernaum

Welcome home!" From a basket of favorite moments, I might just pick this one. It's what I've said to fellow travelers when visiting the land of Jesus' life and ministry. Welcome home. This is the homeland of our faith, the birthplace of our highest hopes. This is the place where Jesus once and for all demonstrated there is no place he won't go to show us how much he loves us.

During Jesus' three years of ministry, he spent a great deal of those few years around the Sea of Galilee. It looks today much the way it appeared then. From its shoreline we can envision Peter walking on water with faltering faith, disciples casting nets, and boats bouncing on storm-tossed waves.

Mustard plants still grow near the shore. Can you imagine Jesus pointing at the tiny yellow seeds and saying, "If you have that much faith, I can work with that"? The real strength of faith is not in the one who has to muster it up but in Christ, who'll take even our little faith and turn it into something powerful.

The same power of Christ that turned waves into walkways, empty nets into breakfast, and chaos into calm is ready to touch our lives with peace.

All it takes is a mustard-seed-sized faith.

CHAPTER 4

CONFRONTING WORRY

I t's two thirty in the morning. You can't sleep. You pound your pillow, adjust the blankets. You roll onto one side, then the other. Nothing works. Everyone else sleeps. Your spouse has taken up residence in dreamland. The dog is curled up in a lump at the foot of your bed. Everyone is asleep. Everyone, that is, except you.

In six hours you'll be walking into a new job, new office, new chapter, new world. You'll be the rookie on the sales team. You are wondering if you made the right decision. The hours are long. The economy is declining. The competition is increasing.

Besides, you are

- twenty-three years old, right out of college, starting your first job;
- thirty-three years old, with two kids to feed and a family to care for;

- forty-three years old, the latest victim of layoffs and downsizing;
- fifty-three years old, not the ideal age to change careers;
- sixty-three years old. What happened to retirement plans and time with the grandkids? Here you are starting over.

No matter the age, questions fall like hailstones. *Will I make enough money? Make any friends? Have a cubicle? Will I be able to learn the software program, the sales pitch, the way to the restroom?*

You feel a twitch in the back of your neck. Suddenly a new strand of anxiety worms its way into your mind. Oh no, a tumor. Just like Granddad. He spent a year in chemotherapy. How will I endure chemo and a new job? Will my insurance cover chemo?

The thoughts rage through your mind like a tornado through a Kansas prairie. They suck any vestige of peace into the sky. The green numbers on the clock are the only lights in your room, indeed the only lights in your life. Another hour passes. You cover your head with a pillow and feel like crying.

What a mess.

What does all this anxiety mean? All this fear? Trepidation? Restlessness? Insecurity? What does it mean?

Simply this: you are a human being.

It does not mean you are emotionally underdeveloped. It does not mean you are stupid, demon possessed, or a failure. It does not mean your parents failed you or vice versa. And, this is important, it does not mean you are not a Christian.

Christians battle anxiety. Jesus battled anxiety, for heaven's sake! In the garden of Gethsemane he prayed three times that he wouldn't have to drink of the cup (Matt. 26:36–44). His heart pumped with such ferocity that capillaries broke and rivulets of crimson streaked down his face (Luke 22:44). He was anxious.

But he didn't stay anxious. He entrusted his fears to his heavenly Father and completed his earthly mission with faith. He will help us do likewise.

"That is why I tell you not to worry about everyday life—whether you have enough food and drink, or enough clothes to wear. Isn't life more than food, and your body more than clothing? Look at the birds. They don't plant or harvest or store food in barns, for your heavenly Father feeds them. And aren't you far more valuable to him than they are? Can all your worries add a single moment to your life?

"And why worry about your clothing? Look at the lilies of the field and how they grow. They don't work or make their clothing, yet Solomon in all his glory was not dressed as beautifully as they are. And if God cares so wonderfully for wildflowers that are here today and thrown into the fire tomorrow, he will certainly care for you. Why do you have so little faith?

"So don't worry about these things, saying, 'What will we eat? What will we drink? What will we wear?' These things dominate the thoughts of unbelievers, but your heavenly Father already knows all your needs. Seek the Kingdom of God above all else, and live righteously, and he will give you everything you need.

"So don't worry about tomorrow, for tomorrow will bring its own worries. Today's trouble is enough for today." (Matt. 6:25–34 NLT)

It's hard to miss the theme of this reading.

"I tell you not to worry about everyday life." (v. 25)

"Can all your worries add a single moment to your life?" (v. 27)

"Why worry?" (v. 28)

"So don't worry about these things." (v. 31)

"So don't worry." (v. 34)

WORRY DOESN'T WORK

Fret won't fill a bird's belly with food or a flower's petal with color. Birds and flowers seem to get along just fine, and they don't take antacids. What's more, you can dedicate a decade of anxious thoughts to your small stature and still not grow one inch. Worry accomplishes nothing.

But still we worry. And now that we know we aren't supposed to worry, we will worry about worrying. So, lest we add anxiety to our list of anxieties, let's be certain what Jesus means when he says "worry."

He's not condemning a healthy concern. A certain level of unease gets us out of bed and on with our responsibilities. It happens to all of us. It happened to me this morning. I awoke at 4:30 a.m., a lurking deadline poking me out of my slumber. Rather than stress out, I chose to get up.

Was my early-morning emotion a sin? My restlessness a mark of an unspiritual heart? I don't think so. My mind was merely doing its job. Manageable doses of anxiety serve as calls to action. Mine was reminding me, warning me, to put the day to good use and not let it slip away. Let's suppose I had responded differently to the early-morning reminder. Rather than tackle the task, I curled up in a fetal position and bemoaned my pathetic state. "The congregation expects too much. Every weekend another sermon. Every sermon another topic . . . Not even Jesus could bear up under such stress. I'll never meet the deadline. When I don't, the staff will hate me, and they'll petition for my dismissal. My firing will embarrass my wife and shame my children. . . . I wonder if we have any Jack Daniels in the house."

Whoa. Legitimate concern has morphed into pathetic panic. I crossed a boundary into a state of fret. I'm no longer anticipating or preparing . . . I've taken up membership in the fraternity of Woe-Be-Me. This is the caution that Jesus gives. He doesn't condemn legitimate concern for responsibility but rather the continuous mindset that dismisses God's presence. Look how one translation renders Jesus' words: "Therefore I tell you, stop being perpetually uneasy (anxious and worried) about your life" (Matt. 6:25 AMPC). There is our definition: perpetual uneasiness over the future. Worry is a state of mind in which God is distrusted and disregarded. An outlook on life that subtracts God from the future faces uncertainties with no faith and tallies up the challenges of the day without entering God into the equation. We pay a high price for such agitation: headaches, loss of sleep, loss of appetite, overeating, irritability, perhaps even high blood pressure, heart disease . . . even cancer. "Do not fret—it only causes harm" (Ps. 37:8 NKJV).

A friend saw an example of "perpetual uneasiness" in his six-year-old daughter. In her hurry to get dressed for school, she tied her shoelaces in a knot. She plopped down at the base of the stairs and fixated her thoughts on the tangled mess. She knew the school bus was coming and the minutes were ticking but gave no thought to the fact that her father was standing nearby willing to help upon request. He watched her grow so anxious that her little hands began to shake and tears began to fall. Finally in an expression of total frustration, she dropped her forehead to her knees and began to sob.

That's the picture of worry. Some people never lift their eyes off their knots. They fixate to the point of frustration, anger, and anxiety, oblivious to the presence of their Father, who stands nearby. My friend finally took it upon himself to come to his daughter's aid. Why didn't the child request her father's help to start with? Good question. Why don't we? Our Father invites us to do so: "Be anxious for nothing, but in everything by prayer and supplication with thanksgiving let your requests be made known to God" (Phil. 4:6 NASB 1995).

This passage douses anxiety like a waterfall on a match. The moment an anxious thought surfaces here is what you do . . . take it to God.

Instead of "Oh no, highway construction. I'll never make it on time," try this: "Highway construction. Lord, will you help me?"

Rather than "I'll never survive the layoffs," say, "God, would you guide me through the layoffs?"

You could lie in bed and stress about the day ahead. Or you could climb out of bed and say, "Thanks, God. Let's get the job done."

Turn every fret into a prayer. Isn't this one of the lessons of the feeding of the multitude?

CHRIST'S CURE FOR WORRY: COUNT TO EIGHT

The hungry crowd appears at an inopportune time. Jesus' heart was heavied by the news of the murder of John the Baptist, so he took the disciples on a retreat. "Come aside by yourselves to a deserted place and rest a while" (Mark 6:31 NKJV).

But then comes the crowd. Droves of people. Fifteen, maybe, twenty thousand individuals. A multitude of misery and sickness bringing nothing but requests. Jesus treats them with kindness. The disciples don't share Jesus' compassion. "That evening the disciples came to him and said, 'This is a remote place, and it's already getting late. Send the crowds away so they can go to the villages and buy food for themselves'" (Matt. 14:15 NLT).

Whoops, somebody is a bit testy. The followers typically preface their comments with the respectful "Lord." Not this time. They issue a command, not a request. They are ready to be done with the people. So they tell Jesus to stop helping them. "Send them home so they can buy food for themselves."

They can defend their opinion. The multitude should have known to pack a meal. Besides, who has the keys to Fort Knox? The disciples don't have resources for such a crowd.

Jesus is not perturbed by their disrespect or lack of compassion;

he simply issues an assignment: "They do not need to go away. You give them something to eat" (v. 16 NKJV).

So they tally their resources and come to a conclusion: "We have here only five loaves and two fish" (v. 17 NKJV).

Can you envision that moment? The followers huddle and take inventory. "Let's count the loaves: one, two, three, four, five. I've got five loaves. Andrew, you check me on this: one, two, three, four, five . . ." Same routine with the fish. No matter how they count it, the bottom line is the same: "only five loaves and two fish." The descriptor *only* stands out as if to say: "Our resources are hopelessly puny. There is nothing left but this wimpy lunch." Phillip adds a personal calculation. "It would take more than half a year's wages to buy enough bread for each one to have a bite!" (John 6:7). The exclamation point is an exasperation point, as if to say, "Your assignment is too great!"

How do you suppose Jesus felt about the basket examination? Do you think he might have wanted them to include the rest of the possibilities? Involve all the options? Do you think he was hoping someone might count to eight?

"Well, let's see. We have five loaves, two fish, and . . . Jesus!" Jesus Christ. The same Jesus who said, "Ask and it will be given to you; seek and you will find; knock and the door will be opened to you" (Luke 11:9).

"If you remain in me and my words remain in you, ask whatever you wish, and it will be done for you" (John 15:7).

"Whatever you ask for in prayer, believe that you have received it, and it will be yours" (Mark 11:24).

Standing next to the disciples was the solution to their

problems . . . but they didn't go to him. They stopped at seven and worried.

Don't do likewise. Count to eight. Better still, count on Christ. The apostles eventually did. Their first act after the resurrection of Jesus was to pray. He'd left them with this challenge: "You shall be witnesses to Me in Jerusalem, and in all Judea and Samaria, and to the end of the earth" (Acts 1:8 NKJV).

The same group who wanted to dismiss the crowd was sent to the world. Did they count the basket contents? Not this time. They chose, instead, to count on Christ. "They went up into the upper room where they were staying . . . [They] all continued with one accord in prayer and supplication" (Acts 1:13–14 NKJV).

You suppose you could learn from their example? I have a few ideas on how you can. Want to count to eight?

EIGHT WORRY STOPPERS

1. **KEEP A WORRY DIARY.** Over a period of days record your anxious thoughts. Maintain a list of all the things that trouble you. Then review them. How many of them turned into reality? You worried that the house would burn down. Did it? That you'd be fired from your job. Were you?

2. **EVALUATE YOUR WORRY CATEGORIES.** Your list will highlight themes of worry. You'll detect recurring areas of pre-occupation that may become obsessions: what people think of you, finances, your appearance, or your performance.

3. **TAKE YOUR WORRIES TO CHRIST.** Imitate the mother

of Jesus at the wedding in Cana. The reception was out of wine, a huge social no-no in the days of Jesus. Mary could have blamed the host for poor planning or the guests for overdrinking, but she didn't mull on the problem. Instead, she took it directly to Jesus. "When they ran out of wine, the mother of Jesus said to Him, 'They have no wine'" (John 2:3 NKJV). When you suffer a shortage of something, see how quickly you can do the same. Our days should be punctuated with such petitions as "I have no wisdom," "I'm running low on patience," "Lord, I'm clean out of options."

4. **LEAVE YOUR WORRIES WITH CHRIST.** "Casting the whole of your care [all your anxieties, all your worries, all your concerns, once and for all] on Him . . ." (1 Peter 5:7 AMPC). Again Mary is our model. When Jesus hesitated at her request, she didn't argue. She told the servants to take their cue from him. No wrangling or wrestling, just trusting.

5. **RECRUIT A WORRY ARMY.** Share your findings with a few loved ones. Ask them to pray with and for you. They're more willing to help than you might imagine. Less worry on your part means more happiness on theirs.

6. **BECOME A WORRY SLAPPER.** Treat frets like mosquitoes. Slap them like the energy-sucking critters they are. The moment a concern surfaces, deal with it. Don't dwell on it. Head worries off before they get the better of you. Don't waste an hour wondering what your boss thinks; ask her. Before you diagnose that mole as cancer, have it examined. Instead of assuming you'll never get out of debt, consult an expert. Be a doer. Not a stewer.

7. **UNDERSTAND GOD'S MANNA PLAN.** He meets daily needs daily. Not weekly or annually. He will not give you a year's

worth of resources today. But he will give you what you need when it is needed. "Let us therefore boldly approach the throne of our gracious God, where we may receive mercy and in his grace find timely help" (Heb. 4:16 NEB). An ancient Dolomite chant expresses the heart that this patient waiting creates.

> Not so in haste my heart!
> Have faith in God, and wait;
> Although He linger long,
> He never comes too late.
>
> He never cometh late;
> He knoweth what is best;
> Vex not thyself in vain;
> Until He cometh, rest.
>
> Until He cometh, rest,
> Nor grudge the hours that roll;
> The feet that wait for God
> Are soonest at the goal.
>
> Are soonest at the goal
> That is not gained with speed;
> Then hold thee still, my heart,
> For I shall wait His lead.[1]

8. **LET GOD BE ENOUGH.** Jesus concludes his call to calmness with this challenge: "Seek first the kingdom of God and His

righteousness, and all these things shall be added to you" (Matt. 6:33 NKJV). Worry disappears as we seek God's kingdom. Seek first the kingdom of wealth, and you'll worry over every dollar. Seek first the kingdom of health, and you'll sweat every pain. Seek first the kingdom of popularity, and you'll relive every conflict. Seek first the kingdom of safety, and you'll jump at every crack of a twig. We worry when we seek less than God and his kingdom.

But when he is enough, then we worry no longer. For he will never leave. About that, we need never worry.

QUESTIONS FOR REFLECTION

1. What worries are you carrying today?
   - How long have these worries weighed on you?
   - How often do you think about them?
   - Max emphasizes that feeling anxious is human. As he said, "It does not mean you are not a Christian" (p. 42). What do you think about this statement?

2. Jesus also felt worried. Scripture describes Jesus' most anxious moments in the garden of Gethsemane. This garden overlooks the walled city of Jerusalem, where Jesus would be put on trial the following day. Read the story in Matthew 26:36–44.
   - How do we know Jesus was having anxious thoughts in the garden?

- What did he do with these thoughts?
- What physical effect did Jesus' anxiety have on him?
- What physical effect does anxiety have on you?
- How does it affect you to know that Jesus felt anxiety too?

3. On the Mount of Beatitudes, Jesus gave a sermon about worry. The Mount of Beatitudes overlooks rolling hills and valleys, lush with green grass and flowers. Keep this in mind as you read Matthew 6:25–34.
   - According to verses 30–34, why shouldn't we worry?
   - Since worry is a natural part of life, how can we know the difference between what Max called "legitimate concern" and "pathetic panic"? (p. 45)
   - When have you felt legitimate concern about something? What did you do as a result?
   - When have you felt pathetic panic? What did you do as a result?

4. Read Philippians 4:6. What should we do with our worries according to this verse?
   - How did the disciples fail to do this with the hungry crowd in Matthew 14?
   - What do you typically do when you start to worry about something?
   - What is one worry you are carrying that you need to hand over to Christ?

5. What are Max's eight worry stoppers?
   - Which one of these worry stoppers could you use to stop the worries you're carrying today?
   - How will you use it?
   - Which one of these worry stoppers could you incorporate into your everyday life so that when worries come up, you know what to do with them?

CHAPTER 5

MAKING FISHERS OF MEN

But the boat was now in the middle of the sea, tossed by the waves, for the wind was contrary. Now in the fourth watch of the night Jesus went to them, walking on the sea. And when the disciples saw Him walking on the sea, they were troubled, saying, "It is a ghost!" And they cried out for fear.

But immediately Jesus spoke to them, saying, "Be of good cheer! It is I; do not be afraid."

And Peter answered Him and said, "Lord, if it is You, command me to come to You on the water."

So He said, "Come." And when Peter had come down out of the boat, he walked on the water to

go to Jesus. But when he saw that the wind was
boisterous, he was afraid; and beginning to sink he
cried out, saying, "Lord, save me!"

And immediately Jesus stretched out His hand
and caught him, and said to him, "O you of little
faith, why did you doubt?" And when they got into
the boat, the wind ceased. (Matt. 14:24–32 NKJV)

The Sea of Galilee can be fickle. As famous lakes go, this is a small one, only thirteen miles at its longest, seven and a half at its widest. The diminutive size makes it more vulnerable to the Golan Heights winds that howl out of the mountains. Low pressure storms turn the lake into a blender, shifting suddenly, blowing first from one direction and then another. Winter months bring such storms every two weeks or so, churning up the waters for two to three days at a time.

Galileans came to expect storms. They were a part of the topography. They still are.

LIFE COMES WITH STORMS

Atmospheric conditions of our fallen world churn serious turbulence. Health crises. Economic struggles. Unwanted invoices and cancer cells that howl down on our lives and turn life into a bull ride.

Peter and his fellow storm riders knew they were in trouble. Sunlight was a distant memory. Rain fell from the night sky in buckets. Lightning sliced the blackness with a silver sword. Winds whipped the sails. The boat lurched and lunged like a kite in a March wind.

"The boat was now in the middle of the sea, tossed by the waves, for the wind was contrary" (Matt. 14:24 NKJV). Descriptive phrase, don't you think? Apt description for the stormy seasons of life. The gusts and the gales turn contrarily against your wishes, leaving you "in the middle of the sea, tossed by the waves."

In the middle of a divorce, tossed about by guilt.

In the middle of debt, tossed about by creditors.

In the middle of a corporate takeover, tossed about by Wall Street and profit margins.

But after as many as nine hours in the sea, the unspeakable happens.

JESUS COMES, COMMANDING THE STORM

The disciples spot someone coming on the water. They assume it's a ghost and cry out from fear. "At about four o'clock in the morning, Jesus came toward them walking on the water. They were scared to death. 'A ghost!' they said, crying out in terror" (vv. 25–26 THE MESSAGE).

They didn't expect Jesus to come to them this way.

Neither did we. We expected him to come in the form of peaceful hymns, or Easter Sundays, or quiet retreats. We expected to find Jesus in morning devotionals, church suppers, and meditation. We never expected to see him in a divorce, death, lawsuit, or jail cell. We never expected to see him in a storm. But it is in storms that he does his finest work, for it is in storms he has our keenest attention.

Jesus replies to their fear with an invitation worthy of inscription on every church cornerstone and archway: "Courage! I am! Don't be afraid!"

I like that translation by Frederick Bruner. More common readings, such as "It is I!" or "I am here!" lose the full force of Jesus' pronouncement. Jesus is not merely announcing his presence on the sea; he is declaring his power over the storm. He's not saying, "I am here." He is saying, *"I am."* He is saying what God said to Moses through the burning bush: "Thus you shall say to the children of Israel, 'I AM has sent me to you'" (Ex. 3:14 NKJV). This is what God said to Abraham in the desert: "I am the LORD" (Gen. 15:7 NKJV) and to the Hebrews in the wilderness: "I am He, and there is no God besides Me" (Deut. 32:39 NKJV).

This is no cry of identity; it is a claim of divinity.

Is anyone in control of these winds? I am.

Who is in charge of the torrent? I am.

Is anyone coming to help? I am.

"Courage! I am! Don't be afraid!" With these words Christ claims the position of Chief Commander of the Storm. Peter, much to his credit, takes Jesus at his word. "Lord, if it is You, command me to come to You on the water" (Matt. 14:28 NKJV).

Peter would rather be out of the boat with Christ than in the boat without him, so he calls on the commander to command. And Jesus does. "So He said, 'Come.' And when Peter had come down out of the boat, he walked on the water to go to Jesus" (v. 29 NKJV).

For a few historic steps and heart-stilling moments, Peter does the impossible. He defies every law of gravity and nature: "he walked on the water to go to Jesus."

I can't help but wonder how Matthew felt as he wrote that sentence. Surely he had to lower his pen and shake his head. "Peter . . . walked on the water to go to Jesus." My editors wouldn't have tolerated such brevity. They would have filled the margin with questions: "Can you elaborate? How quickly did Peter exit the boat? How cautious was his first step? What was the look on his face? Did he step on any fish?"

Matthew has no time for such questions, however; he moves us quickly to the major message of the moment.

WHERE TO STARE IN A STORM

"But when [Peter] saw that the wind was boisterous, he was afraid; and beginning to sink he cried out, saying, 'Lord, save me!'" (v. 30 NKJV).

A wall of water eclipses his view. A wind gust snaps the mast with a crack and a slap. A flash of lightning illuminates the lake and the watery mountain range it has become. Peter shifts his attention away from Jesus and toward the squall, and he sinks like a brick in a pond. Give the storm waters more attention than the Storm Walker, and get ready to do the same.

God wants us to look for good news and seek out the accomplishments of his work.

His call to courage is not a call to naïveté or ignorance. We aren't oblivious to the storms. We just counterbalance them with long looks at God's accomplishments.

"We must pay much closer attention to what we have heard, so that we do not drift away from it" (Heb. 2:1 NASB). Do whatever it takes to keep your gaze on Jesus. Memorize Scripture. Sing hymns. Read biographies of great people. Ponder the testimonies of faithful Christians. Walk to the sound of his voice. Make the deliberate decision to set your hope on him. And when your attention turns away, bring it back. Jeremiah did.

Can we slide to the left on the time line and learn a lesson from this Old Testament prophet? Talk about a person caught in a storm!

> I am the man who has seen affliction
>   under the rod of [God's] wrath;
> he has driven and brought me
>   into darkness without any light;
> surely against me he turns his hand
>   again and again the whole day long.
>
> LAM. 3:1–3 RSV

Jeremiah was depressed. His world collapsed like a sandcastle in a tsunami. He faulted God for his horrible, emotional distress. He also blamed God for his physical ailments.

> He [God] has made my flesh and my skin
>   waste away,
>   and broken my bones; (v. 4 RSV)

His body ached! His heart was sick! His faith was puny.

> [God] has besieged and enveloped me
>> with bitterness and tribulation. (v. 5 RSV)

Jeremiah felt trapped like a man at a dead-end street.

> He has walled me about so that I cannot escape;
>> he has put heavy chains on me;
> though I call and cry for help,
>> he shuts out my prayer;
> he has blocked my ways with hewn stones,
>> he has made my paths crooked. (vv. 7–9 RSV)

Jeremiah thought of nothing but his misery. He could tell you the height of the waves and the speed of the wind. But then he realized how fast he was sinking. So he made a decision that models setting our eyes on God.

> But this I call to mind,
>> and therefore I have hope:
> The steadfast love of the LORD never ceases,
>> his mercies never come to an end;
> they are new every morning;
>> great is thy faithfulness.
> 'The LORD is my portion,' says my soul,
>> 'therefore I will hope in him.'" (vv. 21–24 RSV)

"But this I call to mind . . ." Depressed Jeremiah altered his thoughts, shifted his attention. He turned his eyes away from the waves and looked into the wonder of God.

So did Peter. After a few moments of flailing, he turned back to Christ and cried, "Lord, save me!" (Matt. 14:30 NKJV). Immediately Jesus reached out his hand and caught him. "O you of little faith," he said, "why did you doubt?" And when they climbed into the boat, the wind died down (Matt. 14:31–32 NKJV).

Jesus could have stilled this storm hours earlier. But he didn't. He wanted to teach the followers a lesson.

Jesus could have calmed your storm long ago. But he hasn't. Does he want to teach you a lesson too? He has hung his diplomas in the universe: rainbows, sunsets, horizons, and star-studded skies. He has recorded his accomplishments in Scripture. We're not talking six thousand hours of flight time. His résumé includes the Red Sea opening, lions' mouths closing, Goliath toppling, Lazarus rising, storms stilling, and sea strollings.

His lesson is clear. Are you scared in the storm? Then don't stare at the storm. Stare at him. This may be your first flight. But it's not his.

PARABOLIC DISCOURSE

Want to give every day a chance?

Jesus says, give the grace you've been given.

Take a long look at his reply to Peter's question: "'Lord, how often should I forgive someone who sins against me? Seven times?'

'No, not seven times,' Jesus replied, 'but seventy times seven!'"
(Matt. 18:21–22 NLT).

God forgives the unforgivable.

> Therefore, the Kingdom of Heaven can be compared to a king
> who decided to bring his accounts up to date with servants
> who had borrowed money from him. In the process, one of his
> debtors was brought in who owed him millions of dollars. He
> couldn't pay, so his master ordered that he be sold—along with
> his wife, his children, and everything he owned—to pay the
> debt. (Matt. 18:23–25 NLT)

Such an immense debt. More literal translations say the servant
owed 10,000 talents. One talent equaled 6,000 denarii. One denarius equaled one day's wage (Matt. 20:2). One talent, then, would
equate to 6,000 days' worth of work. Ten thousand talents would
represent 60 million days or more than 164,000 years of labor. A
person earning $100 a day would owe $600 million.

Whoa! What an astronomical sum. Jesus employs hyperbole,
right? He's exaggerating to make a point. Or is he? One person
would never owe such an amount to another. But might Jesus be
referring to the debt we owe to God?

Let's calculate our indebtedness to him. How often do you sin,
hmm, in an hour? To sin is to "fall short" (Rom. 3:23). Worry is
falling short on faith. Impatience is falling short on kindness. The
critical spirit falls short on love. How often do you come up short
with God? For the sake of discussion let's say ten times an hour
and tally the results. Ten sins an hour times sixteen waking hours

(assuming we don't sin in our sleep) times 365 days a year, times the average male life span of seventy-four years. I'm rounding the total off at 4.3 million sins per person.

Tell me, how do you plan to pay God for your 4.3 million sin increments? Your payout is unachievable. Unreachable. You're swimming in a Pacific Ocean of debt. Jesus' point precisely. The debtor in the story? You and me. The king? God. Look at what God does.

> He [the servant] couldn't pay, so his master ordered that he be sold—along with his wife, his children, and everything he owned—to pay the debt. But the man fell down before his master and begged him, "Please, be patient with me, and I will pay it all." Then his master was filled with pity for him, and he released him and forgave his debt. (Matt. 18:25–27 NLT)

God pardons the zillion sins of selfish humanity. Forgives sixty million sin-filled days. "Out of sheer generosity he put us in right standing with himself. A pure gift. He got us out of the mess we're in and restored us to where he always wanted us to be. And he did it by means of Jesus Christ" (Rom. 3:24 THE MESSAGE).

God forgives the unforgivable. Were this the only point of the story, we'd have ample points to ponder. But this is only Act 1 of the two-act play. The punch line is yet to come.

We do the unthinkable.

The forgiven refuse to forgive.

> But when the man left the king, he went to a fellow servant who owed him a few thousand dollars. He grabbed him by the throat

and demanded instant payment. His fellow servant fell down before him and begged for a little more time. "Be patient with me, and I will pay it," he pleaded. But his creditor wouldn't wait. He had the man arrested and put in prison until the debt could be paid in full. (Matt. 18:28–30 NLT)

Incomprehensible behavior. Multimillion-dollar forgiveness should produce a multimillion-dollar forgiver, shouldn't it? The forgiven servant can forgive a petty debt, can't he? This one doesn't. Note, he won't wait (18:30). He refuses to forgive. He could have. He should have. The forgiven should forgive. Which makes us wonder, did this servant truly accept the king's forgiveness?

Something is missing from this story. Gratitude. Notably absent from the parable is the joy of the forgiven servant. Like the nine ungrateful lepers, this man never tells the king "thank you." He offers no words of appreciation, sings no song of celebration. His life has been spared, his family liberated, his sentence lifted, a titanic debt forgiven—and he says nothing. He should be hosting a Thanksgiving Day parade. He begs for mercy like a student on the brink of flunking out of college. But once he receives it, he acts as if he never scored less than a B.

Could his silence make the loudest point of the parable? "He who is forgiven little, loves little" (Luke 7:47 RSV). This man loves little apparently because he had received little grace.

You know who I think this guy is? A grace rejecter. He never accepts the grace of the king. He leaves the throne room with a sly smirk, as one who dodged a bullet, found a loophole, worked the system, pulled a fast one. He talked his way out of a jam. He bears the mark of the unforgiven—he refuses to forgive.

When the king hears about the servant's stingy heart, he blows his crown. He goes cyclonic:

> "You wicked servant! I forgave you all that debt because you begged me. Should you not also have had compassion on your fellow servant, just as I had pity on you?" And his master was angry, and delivered him to the torturers until he should pay all that was due to him. So My heavenly Father also will do to you if each of you, from his heart, does not forgive his brother his trespasses. (Matt. 18:32–35 NKJV)

The curtain falls on Act 2, and we are left to ponder the principles of the story. The big one comes quickly. *The grace-given give grace.* Forgiven people forgive people. The mercy-marinated drip mercy. "God is kind to you so you will change your hearts and lives" (Rom. 2:4 NCV).

Before her conversion to Christ, she endlessly nagged, picked on, and berated her husband. When she became a Christian, nothing changed. She kept nagging. Finally he told her, "I don't mind that you were born again. I just wish you hadn't been born again as yourself."

One questions if the wife was born again to start with. Apple trees bear apples, wheat stalks produce wheat, and forgiven people forgive people. Grace is the natural outgrowth of grace.

The forgiven who won't forgive can expect a sad fate—a life full of many bad and bitter days. The "master . . . delivered him to the torturers until he should pay all that was due to him" (Matt. 18:34 NKJV).

In the end we all choose what lives inside us. May you choose forgiveness.

Life comes with voices. Voices lead to choices. Choices have consequences.

Why do some Christians grumble at the picnic? Why do some saints thrive while others scramble to survive? Why do some tackle Everest-size challenges and succeed while others walk seemingly downhill paths and stumble? Why are some people unquenchably content while others are inexplicably unhappy?

I've wondered this in my own life. Some seasons feel like a downhill, downwind bike ride. Others are like pedaling a flat-tired unicycle up Pikes Peak. Why?

Glory days happen when we make good choices. Trouble happens when we don't. This is the headline message delivered by Joshua when he assembled his people in the Valley of Shechem.

The key geographical touchstones in the book of Joshua point to God's power and empowerment of his people. The list includes . . .

- the Jordan River (site of the crossing);
- the Gilgal encampment (the stones of remembrance and renewal of circumcision);
- Jericho (where Joshua saw the Commander and the walls fell);
- Ai (where Achan fell and Joshua rebounded);
- and now Shechem.

The pilgrimage to Shechem was Moses' idea (Deut. 27:4–8). He had instructed Joshua to bring the invasion to a halt and every person to the Valley of Shechem. Shechem was a twenty-mile hike from the Hebrew encampment at Gilgal.[1] The Hebrews must have looked like an Amazon River of humanity as they marched.

Once they reached the valley, Joshua set about the task of building an altar.

> Now Joshua built an altar to the LORD God of Israel in Mount Ebal, as Moses the servant of the LORD had commanded the children of Israel, as it is written in the Book of the Law of Moses: "an altar of whole stones over which no man has wielded an iron tool." And they offered on it burnt offerings to the LORD, and sacrificed peace offerings. And there, in the presence of the children of Israel, he wrote on the stones a copy of the law of Moses, which he had written. (Josh. 8:30–32 NKJV)

In the ancient Near East it was customary for kings to commemorate their military achievements by recording their conquests on huge stones covered with plaster. Joshua, however, didn't memorialize his work. He celebrated God's law. The secret to the successful campaign of the Hebrews was not the strength of the army but the resolve of the people to keep God's commandments.

And then the best part:

> Then all Israel, with their elders and officers and judges, stood on either side of the ark before the priests, the Levites, who

bore the ark of the covenant of the LORD, the stranger as well as he who was born among them. Half of them were in front of Mount Gerizim and half of them in front of Mount Ebal, as Moses the servant of the LORD had commanded before, that they should bless the people of Israel. And afterward he read all the words of the law, the blessings and the cursings, according to all that is written in the Book of the Law. (vv. 33–34 NKJV)

The meadows of Shechem sit between Mount Ebal and Mount Gerizim. Gardens, orchards, and olive groves grow throughout the valley. Limestone stratum sits in the deepest part of the crevice, broken into ledges "so as to present the appearance of a series of regular benches."[2] The rock formation creates an amphitheater with acoustic properties that allow a sound originating on one side of the valley to be heard on the other.

The tribes were assigned their places: six on one side and six on the other. Midway between stood the priests, Levites, leaders, and the ark of the covenant. When Joshua and the Levites read the blessings, the tribes standing on Gerizim shouted, "Amen!" When the leaders read the curses, the million or so people on Ebal declared, "Amen!"[3]

Can you imagine the drama of the moment?

"If you listen obediently to the voice of God, he will . . .

"defeat your enemies!"

"Amen!"

"order a blessing on your barns!"

"Amen!"

"lavish you with good things!"

"Amen!"

"throw open the doors of his sky vaults and pour rain on your land" (Deut. 28:1–13).

"Amen!"

The proclamation of the curses followed the same pattern. "Cursed is anyone who . . .

"carves a god image!"

"Amen!"

"demeans a parent!"

"Amen!"

"takes a bribe to kill an innocent person."

"Amen!" (Deut. 27).

Back and forth, back and forth. Voices reverberated off the stone cliffs. All the people—children, immigrants, old-timers, everyone—in antiphonal rhythm proclaimed their values. "There was not a word of all that Moses had commanded which Joshua did not read before all the assembly of Israel, with the women, the little ones, and the strangers who were living among them" (Josh. 8:35 NKJV).

Keep in mind the when and where of this assembly. When did this event happen? In the midst of an invasion. Where? Smack-dab in the middle of enemy territory. These desert-toughened people pressed the Pause button on the physical battle in order to fight the spiritual one.

Heeding God's Word is more critical than fighting God's war. Indeed, heeding God's Word *is* fighting God's war. Conquest happens as the covenant is honored.

Do you want a promised-land life?

Desire the fullness of glory days?

Want to experience Canaan to the fullest?

Obey God's commands.

What's that? You expected something more mystical, exotic, intriguing? You thought that the Canaan-level life was birthed from ecstatic utterances or angelic visions, mountaintop moments, or midnight messages from heaven?

Sorry to disappoint you. "Obedience," wrote C. S. Lewis, "is the key to all doors."[4] Don't think for a second that you can heed the wrong voice, make the wrong choice, and escape the consequences.

At the same time obedience leads to a waterfall of goodness, not just for you, but for your children, children's children, great-grandchildren, and the children of a thousand generations in the future. God promises to show "love to a thousand generations of those who love me and keep my commandments" (Ex. 20:6).

As we obey God's commands, we open the door for God's favor.

Obedience leads to blessing. Disobedience leads to trouble.

Remember Jesus' parable about the two builders who each built a house? One built on cheap, easy-to-access sand. The other built on costly, difficult-to-reach rock. The second construction project demanded more time and expense, but when the spring rains turned the creek into a gully washer, guess which builder enjoyed a blessing and which experienced trouble? Beachfront property isn't worth much if it can't withstand the storm.

According to Jesus the wise builder is "whoever hears these sayings of Mine, and does them" (Matt. 7:24 NKJV). Both builders heard the teachings. The difference between the two was not knowledge and ignorance but obedience and disobedience. Security comes as we put God's precepts into practice. We're only as strong as our obedience. "Be doers of the word, and not hearers only, deceiving yourselves" (James 1:22 NKJV).

Remember who you are; you are God's child. You've been bought by the most precious commodity in the history of the universe: the blood of Christ. You are indwelled by the Spirit of the living God. You are being equipped for an eternal assignment that will empower you to live in the very presence of God. You have been set apart for a holy calling. You are his.

Remember where you are; this is Canaan. You are in the promised land, not geographically but spiritually. This is the land of grace and hope and freedom and truth and love and life. The devil has no jurisdiction over you. He acts as if he does. He walks with a swagger and brings temptation, but as you resist him and turn to God, he must flee (James 4:7).

Decide now what you will say when temptation presents itself.

Choose obedience. And, as you do, you can expect blessings: the blessing of a clean conscience, the blessing of a good night's sleep, the blessing of God's fellowship, the blessing of God's favor. This is no guarantee of an easy life. It is the assurance of God's help. "The good man does not escape all troubles—he has them too. But the Lord helps him in each and every one" (Ps. 34:19 TLB).

One final thought before we leave the Valley of Shechem. Take note of the altar's location. The altar made with unhewed stone—where was it built? Not on Gerizim, the mount of blessing. Joshua built it on Ebal, the hill of the cursing. Even in the midst of poor choices, there is grace.

May we hear the right voice. May we make the right choice. May we enjoy blessing upon blessing.

But if we don't, may we return to the altar on Ebal. It was built for people like us.

QUESTIONS FOR REFLECTION

1. What is unique about the location and size of the Sea of Galilee? Consider this as you read Matthew 14:24–32.
   - What kind of storm were the disciples experiencing?
   - What storms in life have tossed you around like the disciples in the boat?
   - What did Jesus say to the disciples when he appeared to them on the Sea of Galilee?
   - When has Jesus showed up in the middle of your storm?
   - How did Christ's presence in that moment affect you or your circumstance?

2. When did Peter begin to sink into the water?
   - When you're in one of life's storms, what is your focus?
   - What would change if you focused on Jesus instead?

3. While Jesus and his disciples were in Capernaum, a major center of trade on the northern shore of the Sea of Galilee,

he told them a parable about forgiveness. (You can read the full parable in Matthew 18:21–35.)

- Considering the location where Jesus told this parable—a trading town with merchants and businessmen—how do you think Jesus' audience would have connected to this story?
- How did the man whose debts had been forgiven by his master react to that gift?
- How do you feel about God's forgiveness toward you? Do you believe he has forgiven you? Why or why not?
- How does this belief affect the way you forgive, or struggle to forgive, others and yourself?

4. In the midst of battle Joshua led the Hebrews into the Valley of Shechem to "read all the words of the law—the blessings and the curses—just as it is written in the Book of the Law" (Josh. 8:34).

- How is this valley uniquely suited for a communal reading of God's Word?
- What role does God's Word play in your life today?
- How could obedience to God's Word help you in whatever battle or storm you are facing?
- Consider writing a favorite scripture on a stone, as Joshua did. Place it where you'll see it daily as a reminder.
- Think about your scripture stone: why you chose it, what it means in your walk with the Lord, and how it strengthens your faith.

CHAPTER 6

TEACHING, TEACHING, TEACHING

The world can seem dark.

Downtown streets darkened with anger and hate. Innocents trafficked, innocence lost. Homeless, jobless. Pandemic and dread. A society worn out, worked up, and wondering what comes next.

I wonder what the world will hold for my grandchildren. Their greatest concerns today are finding lightning bugs on a summer night or learning to share with their siblings. Would that their world would always be so innocent. It won't. Forests shadow every trail, and cliffs edge every turn. Every life has its share of fear. My grandchildren are no exception.

Nor are your children and grandchildren. And as appealing as a desert island or a monastery might be, seclusion is simply not the answer for facing a scary tomorrow.

Then what is? Does someone have a hand on the throttle of this train, or has the engineer bailed out just as we come in sight of dead man's curve?

I may have found part of the answer in, of all places, the first chapter of the New Testament. I've often thought it strange that Matthew would begin his book with a genealogy. Certainly not good journalism. A list of who sired whom wouldn't get past most editors.

But then again, Matthew wasn't a journalist, and the Holy Spirit wasn't trying to get our attention. He was making a point. God had promised he would give a Messiah through the bloodline of Abraham (Gen. 12:3), and he did.

"Having doubts about the future?" Matthew asks. "Just take a look at the past." And with that he opens the cedar chest of Jesus' lineage and begins pulling out the dirty laundry.

He begins with Abraham, the father of the nation, who more than once lied like Pinocchio just to save his neck (Gen. 12:10–20).

Abraham's grandson Jacob was deceitful. He cheated his brother, lied to his father, got swindled, and then swindled his uncle (Gen. 27, 30).

Jacob's son Judah was so blinded by testosterone that he engaged the services of a streetwalker, not knowing she was his daughter-in-law! When he learned her identity, he threatened to have her burned to death for solicitation (Gen. 38).

Special mention is made of Solomon's mother, Bathsheba (who bathed in questionable places), and Solomon's father, David, who watched her bathe (2 Sam. 11:2–3).

Rahab was a harlot (Josh. 2:1). Ruth was a foreigner (Ruth 1:4).

Manasseh made the list, even though he forced his son to walk through fire (2 Kings 21:6). His son Amon is on the list, even though he rejected God (2 Kings 21:22).

Seems that almost half the kings were crooks, half were embezzlers, and all but a handful worshiped an idol or two for good measure.

And so reads the list of Jesus' not-so-great great-grandparents. Seems like the only common bond among this lot was a promise. A promise from heaven that God would use them to send his Son.

Why did God use these people? Didn't have to. Could have just laid the Savior on a doorstep. Would have been simpler that way. And why does God tell us their stories? Why does God give us an entire testament of the blunders and stumbles of his people?

Simple. He knew what you and I watched on the news last night. He knew you would fret. He knew I would worry. And he wants us to know that when the world goes wild, he stays calm.

Want proof? Read the last name on the list. In spite of all the crooked halos and tasteless gambols of his people, the last name on the list is the first one promised—Jesus.

"Joseph was the husband of Mary, and Mary was the mother of Jesus. Jesus is called the Christ" (Matt. 1:16 NCV).

Period. No more names are listed. No more are needed. As if God is announcing to a doubting world, "See, I did it. Just as I said I would. The plan succeeded."

The famine couldn't starve it.

Four hundred years of Egyptian slavery couldn't oppress it.

Wilderness wanderings couldn't lose it.

Babylonian captivity couldn't stop it.

Clay-footed pilgrims couldn't spoil it.

The promise of the Messiah threads its way through forty-two generations of rough-cut stones, forming a necklace fit for the King who came. Just as promised.

And the promise remains.

"Those people who keep their faith until the end will be saved," Joseph's child assures (Matt. 24:13 NCV).

"In this world you will have trouble, but be brave! I have defeated the world" (John 16:33 NCV).

God keeps his promise.

See for yourself. In the manger. He's there.

See for yourself. In the tomb. He's gone.

MULTITUDES DRAWN TO CHRIST

When we obey God, we naively believe that peace always follows obedience.

I always think about the disciples when I think about young missionaries. The disciples only did what they were told. Jesus told them to get into the boat, so they did. They didn't question the order; they simply obeyed it. They could have objected. After all, it was evening and darkness was only minutes away.

What was the result of their obedience? John's crisp description will tell you: "That evening Jesus' followers went down to Lake Galilee. It was dark now, and Jesus had not yet come to them. The followers got into a boat and started across the lake to Capernaum. By now a strong wind was blowing, and the waves on the lake were getting bigger" (John 6:16–18 NCV).

What a chilling phrase—"Jesus had not yet come to them." Caught in the storm of the "not yet." They had done exactly what Jesus said, and look what it got them—a night on a storm-tossed sea with their Master somewhere on the shore.

It's one thing to suffer for doing wrong. Something else entirely to suffer for doing right. But it happens. And when the storm bursts, it washes away the naive assumption that if I do right, I will never suffer.

And so the winds blow.

And so the boat bounces.

And so the disciples wonder, *Why the storm, and where is Jesus?* It's bad enough to be in the storm, but to be in the storm alone?

The disciples had been on the sea for about nine hours.[1] John tells us they rowed three or four miles (John 6:19). That's a long night. How many times did they search the darkness for their Master? How many times did they call out his name?

Why did he take so long?

Why does he take so long?

Mark tells us that during the storm Jesus "saw his followers struggling" (Mark 6:48 NCV). Through the night he saw them. Through the storm he saw them. And like a loving father he waited. He waited until the right time, until the right moment. He waited until he knew it was time to come, and then he came.

What made it the right time? I don't know. Why was the ninth hour better than the fourth or fifth? I can't answer that. Why does

God wait until the money is gone? Why does he wait until the sickness has lingered? Why does he choose to wait until the other side of the grave to answer the prayers for healing?

I don't know. I only know his timing is always right. I can only say he will do what is best. "God will always give what is right to his people who cry to him night and day, and he will not be slow to answer them" (Luke 18:7 NCV).

Though you hear nothing, he is speaking. Though you see nothing, he is acting. With God there are no accidents. Every incident is intended to bring us closer to him.

Can I give a great example? The direct route from Egypt to Israel would take only eleven days by foot.[2] But God took the Israelites on the long road, which took forty years. Why did he do that? Read carefully the explanation.

> Remember how the LORD your God has led you in the desert for these forty years, taking away your pride and testing you, because he wanted to know what was in your heart. . . . He took away your pride when he let you get hungry, and then he fed you with manna, which neither you nor your ancestors had ever seen. This was to teach you that a person does not live on bread alone, but by everything the LORD says. During these forty years, your clothes did not wear out, and your feet did not swell. Know in your heart that the LORD your God corrects you as a parent corrects a child. (Deut. 8:2–5 NCV)

Look what God did in the desert. He took away the Israelites' pride. He tested their hearts. He proved that he would provide for them. Did God want the children of Israel to reach the promised land? Of course. But he was more concerned that they arrive prepared than that they arrive soon.

So what does God do while we are enduring the pain? What does he do while we are in the storm? You'll love this. He prays for us. Jesus wasn't in the boat because he had gone to the hills to pray (Mark 6:46). Jesus prayed. That is remarkable. It is even more remarkable that Jesus didn't stop praying when his disciples were struggling. When he heard their cries, he remained in prayer.

Why? Two possible answers. Either he didn't care, or he believed in prayer. I think you know the correct choice.

And you know what? Jesus hasn't changed. He still prays for his disciples. "Because Jesus lives forever, he will never stop serving as priest. So he is able always to save those who come to God through him because he always lives, asking God to help them" (Heb. 7:24–25 NCV).

So where does that leave us? While Jesus is praying and we are in the storm, what are we to do? Simple. We do what the disciples did. We row. The disciples rowed most of the night. Mark says they were "struggling hard" to row the boat (Mark 6:48 NCV). The word *struggle* is elsewhere translated as "tormented." Wasn't easy. Wasn't glamorous.

Much of life is spent rowing. Getting out of bed. Fixing lunches. Turning in assignments. Changing diapers. Paying bills. Routine. Regular. More struggle than strut. More wrestling than resting.

Don't give up! Don't lay down the oars! He is too wise to forget you, too loving to hurt you. When you can't see him, trust him. He is praying a prayer that he himself will answer.

Sometimes the trials and tribulations make retaliation seem appealing. But Jesus has a better idea.

John 13 records the events of the final night before Jesus' death. He and his followers had gathered in the upper room for Passover. John begins his narrative with a lofty statement: "Jesus knew that the Father had given him authority over everything and that he had come from God and would return to God" (John 13:3 NLT).

Jesus knew the who and why of his life. Who was he? God's Son. Why was he on earth? To serve the Father. Jesus knew his identity and authority, "so he got up from the table, took off his robe, wrapped a towel around his waist, and poured water into a basin. Then he began to wash the disciples' feet, drying them with the towel he had around him" (John 13:4–5 NLT).

Jesus—CEO, head coach, king of the world, sovereign of the seas—washed feet.

This was the job of a servant. When the master came home from a day spent walking the cobblestone streets, he expected a foot washing. The lowliest servant met him at the door with towel and water.

But in the upper room there was no servant.

Jesus didn't exclude a single follower, though we wouldn't have faulted him had he bypassed Philip. When Jesus told the disciples to feed the throng of five thousand hungry people, Philip, in effect, had retorted, "It's impossible!" (John 6:7). So what does Jesus do with someone who questions his commands? Apparently he washes the doubter's feet.

James and John lobbied for cabinet-level positions in Christ's kingdom. So what does Jesus do when people use his kingdom for personal advancement? He slides a basin in their direction.

Peter quit trusting Christ in the storm. He tried to talk Christ out of going to the cross. Within hours Peter would curse the very name of Jesus and hightail his way into hiding. In fact, all twenty-four of Jesus' followers' feet would soon scoot, leaving Jesus to face his accusers alone. Do you ever wonder what God does with promise breakers? He washes their feet.

Most people won't do that. Most people keep a pot of anger on low boil.

But you aren't "most people." Grace has happened to you. Look at your feet. They are wet, grace soaked. Your toes and arches and heels have felt the cool basin of God's grace. Jesus has washed the grimiest parts of your life. He didn't bypass you and carry the basin toward someone else. Can't you share your grace with others?

"Since I, your Lord and Teacher, have washed your feet, you ought to wash each other's feet. I have given you an example to follow. Do as I have done to you" (John 13:14–15 NLT).

To accept grace is to accept the vow to give it.

Harbored grudges suck the joy out of life. Revenge won't paint the blue back in your sky or restore the spring in your step.

It will leave you bitter, bent, and angry. Give the grace you've been given.

You don't endorse the deeds of your offender when you do. Jesus didn't endorse your sins by forgiving you.

Grace is not blind. It sees the hurt full well. But grace chooses to see God's forgiveness even more. It refuses to let hurts poison the heart. "See to it that no one falls short of the grace of God and that no bitter root grows up to cause trouble and defile many" (Heb. 12:15). Where grace is lacking, bitterness abounds. Where grace abounds, forgiveness grows.

Sequence matters. Jesus washes first; we wash next. He demonstrates; we follow. He uses the towel and then extends it to us, saying, "Now you do it. Walk across the floor of your upper room and wash the feet of your Judas."

So go ahead. Get your feet wet. Remove your socks and shoes, and set your feet in the basin. First one, then the other. Let the hands of God wipe away every dirty part of your life.

Forgiveness may not happen all at once. But it can happen with you. After all, you have wet feet.

QUESTIONS FOR REFLECTION

1. Jesus' human story begins in Bethlehem, but his lineage, detailed in the first chapter of Matthew's gospel, began long before that with ancestors such as Abraham in Ur, David in Jerusalem, and Rahab in Jericho—a long list of what Max called "not-so-great grandparents."

   - What imperfections do you have in your family history? What effect has that had on you or your family?
   - What does Max say is the purpose of Matthew's opening his gospel in this way?
   - How could this encourage you, considering your family's imperfect history as well as your own?

2. We revisited the storm on the Sea of Galilee in this chapter.
   Read the story again in John 6:16–21. The disciples had
   obeyed Jesus, who told them to cross the sea and go to the
   city of Capernaum. Yet, they found themselves in a storm.
   - Describe a time you obeyed God only to find yourself
     in a storm.
   - How did this affect your faith?
   - Where was Jesus when the disciples were rowing
     through the storm?
   - When did he eventually appear to them?
   - What does this tell you about where Jesus was in
     storms you've weathered in the past or where he is if
     you are weathering one today?

3. When the Israelites were freed from slavery in Egypt, where
   did God direct them to go?
   - Why did he take them this way?
   - When has God led you on an indirect route to a final
     destination he had planned for you?
   - How did he provide for you on this journey?
   - How did this journey prepare you for what you
     faced next?

4. As you wait for a storm in your life to subside or as you wait
   to arrive at a destination you know God has promised you,
   how can you keep "rowing"?

5. Jesus shared the Passover meal with his disciples the night before his crucifixion. They ate in what is traditionally called the upper room, a room in a home located in Jerusalem, where many people had come to celebrate Passover.

    - What did Jesus do for the disciples in the upper room?
    - Think about someone who has hurt or betrayed you. How would it feel to serve that person by washing his or her feet?
    - How would it feel to be in the upper room with Jesus that night and let him wash your feet, knowing you've sinned and betrayed him?
    - How could you show grace to the person you mentioned earlier or to another person who has hurt you?

CHAPTER 7

PERFORMING
MIRACLES

D o you think he can?"
"Do you think he cares?"
"Do you think he'll come?"

The questions emerge from the mother's heart. Fear drapes her words and shadows her face.

Her husband stops at the door of their house and looks back into her tired, frightened eyes, then over her shoulder at the figure of his sick daughter lying on the pallet. The girl shivers from the fever. The mother shakes from the fear. The father shrugs in desperation and answers, "I don't know what he'll do, but I don't know what else to do."

The crowd outside the house parts to let the father pass. They would on any day. He is the city leader. But they do this today because his daughter is dying.

"Bless you, Jairus," one offers. But Jairus doesn't stop. He hears only the questions of his wife.

"Do you think he can?"

"Do you think he cares?"

"Do you think he'll come?"

Jairus steps quickly down the path through the fishing village of Capernaum. The size of the following crowd increases with every person he passes. They know where Jairus is going. They know whom he seeks. Jairus goes to the shore to seek Jesus. As they near the water's edge, they spot the teacher encircled by a multitude. A citizen steps ahead to clear a trail, announcing the presence of the synagogue ruler. Villagers comply. The Red Sea of humanity parts, leaving a people-walled path. Jairus wastes no seconds. "When he saw Jesus, he fell to his knees, beside himself as he begged, 'My dear daughter is at death's door. Come and lay hands on her so she will get well and live.' Jesus went with him, the whole crowd tagging along, pushing and jostling him" (Mark 5:23–24 THE MESSAGE).

Jesus' instant willingness moistens the eyes of Jairus. For the first time in a long time, a sunray lands on the father's soul. He all but runs as he leads Jesus back to the path toward home. Jairus dares to believe he is moments from a miracle.

Jesus can help.

Jesus does care.

Jesus will come.

People scatter out of the way and step in behind. Servants rush ahead to inform Jairus's wife. But then, just as suddenly as Jesus came, Jesus stops. Jairus, unaware, takes a dozen more steps before he realizes he's walking alone. The people stopped when

Jesus did. And everyone is trying to make sense of Jesus' question: "Who touched my clothes?" (v. 30). The sentence triggers a rush of activity. Heads turn toward each other. Disciples respond to Christ. Someone moves back so someone else can come forward.

Jairus can't see who. And, quite frankly, he doesn't care who. Precious seconds are passing. His precious daughter is passing. Moments ago he grand marshaled the Hope Parade. Now he stands on the outside looking in and feels his fragile faith unravel. He looks toward his house and back at Christ and wonders afresh:

I wonder if he can.

I wonder if he cares.

I wonder if he'll come.

We know the questions of Jairus because we've faced the fear of Jairus. His Capernaum is our hospital, courthouse, or lonely highway. His dying daughter is our dying marriage, career, future, or friend. Jairus is not alone in asking Jesus for a miracle.

We've done the same. With belief weighing a feather more than unbelief, we've fallen at Jesus' feet and begged. He replies with hope. His answer couriers fresh light. The cloud parts. The sun shines . . . for a time.

But halfway to the miracle, Jesus stops. The illness returns, the heart hardens, the factory closes, the check bounces, the criticism resumes, and we find ourselves like Jairus, on the outside looking in, feeling like a low item on God's to-do list, wondering if Jesus remembers. Wondering if he can, cares, or comes.

Jairus feels a touch on his shoulder. He turns to look into the pale face of a sad servant who tells him, "Your daughter is dead. Why bother the teacher anymore?" (v. 35).

It's fallen to me on a few occasions to fulfill the task of this servant. To bear death tidings. I've informed a father of the death of his teenage son, my siblings of the death of our dad, more than one child of the death of a parent.

Each announcement is met with silence. Wailing or fainting may soon follow, but the first response is a shock-soaked silence. As if no heart can receive the words and no words can express the heart. No one knows what to say to death.

Was it into such a silence that Jesus urged, "Don't be afraid; just believe" (v. 36)?

Believe? Jairus might have thought, *Believe what? Believe how? Believe whom? My daughter is dead. My wife is distraught. And you, Jesus, well, Jesus, you are late. Had you come when I asked, followed when I led . . . Why did you let my little girl die?*

Jairus had no way of knowing the answer. But we do. Why did Jesus let the girl die? So that two thousand years' worth of strugglers would hear Jesus' response to human tragedy. To all who have stood where Jairus stood and asked what Jairus asked, Jesus says, "Don't be afraid; just believe."

Believe that he can. Believe that he is able to help.

Note how the story takes a sudden turn. Until this point Jesus has followed the lead of Jairus. Now he takes control. He commandeers the scene. He trims his team down to fighting size: "And He permitted no one to follow Him except Peter, James, and John the brother of James" (Mark 5:37 NKJV).

Jesus tells the mourners to clam up. "When He came in, He said to them, 'Why make this commotion and weep? The child is not dead, but sleeping'" (Mark 5:39 NKJV).

Then they mock him, "he put them all out" (v. 40). The English translation softens the action. The Greek uses a bare-knuckled verb—*ekballo, which* means to cast out or throw out. Jesus, the temple cleanser and demon-caster, rolls up his sleeves. He's the sheriff in the rowdy saloon placing one hand on shirt collar and the other on trouser belt and tossing the troublemaking doubt stirrers into the street.

He then turns his attention to the body of the girl. He bears the confidence of Einstein adding two plus two, Beethoven playing "Chopsticks," Ben Hogan approaching a one-inch putt. Can Jesus call the dead to life? Of course he can.

But does he care? Might he be mighty and tender? Have muscle and mercy? Does the plight of a twelve-year-old girl in Podunkville appear on the radar screen of heaven?

An earlier moment in the story reveals the answer. It's subtle. You might have missed it. "As soon as Jesus heard the word that was spoken, He said to the ruler of the synagogue, 'Do not be afraid; only believe'" (v. 36 NKJV).

Jesus heard the servant's words. No one had to tell him about the girl's death. Though separated from Jairus, occupied with the case of the woman, and encircled by pressing villagers, Jesus never took his ear off the girl's father. Jesus was listening the entire time. He heard. He cared. He cared enough to speak into Jairus's fear, to come into Jairus's home.

> He took the father and the mother of the child, and those who were with Him, and entered where the child was lying. Then He took the child by the hand, and said to her, "Talitha, cumi,"

which is translated, "Little girl, I say to you, arise." Immediately the girl arose and walked. (vv. 40–42 NKJV)

A pronouncement from the path would have worked. A declaration from afar would have awakened the girl's heart. But Jesus wanted to do more than raise the dead. He wanted to show that he not only can and cares, but he comes.

Into the houses of Jairuses. Into the world of his children. He comes to the small as Mary's baby and to the poor as a carpenter's boy. He comes to the young as a Nazarene teenager and to the forgotten as an unnoticed kid in an obscure village. He comes to the busy as the oldest son of a large family, to the stressed as the leader of restless disciples, to the tired as one with no pillow for his head.

He comes to all. He speaks to all. He still urges:

"Don't be afraid; just believe."

Believe that he can, believe that he comes, believe that he cares. Oh, how we need to believe. Fear pillages so much peace from our days.

When ancient sailors sketched maps of the oceans, they disclosed their fears. On the vast unexplored waters, geographers wrote words such as these:

"Here be dragons."

"Here be demons."

"Here be sirens."

Were a map drawn of your world, would we read such phrases? Over the unknown waters of adulthood, "Here be dragons." Near the sea of the empty nest, "Here be demons." Next to the furthermost latitudes of death and eternity, do we read, "Here be sirens"?

Mark it down. You will never go where God is not. You may be transferred, enlisted, commissioned, reassigned, or hospitalized, but—brand this truth on your heart—you can never go where God is not. "I am with you always," Jesus promised (Matt. 28:20 NKJV).

Don't be afraid; just believe.

The presence of fear does not mean you have no faith. Fear visits everyone. Even Christ was afraid (Mark 14:33). But make your fear a visitor and not a resident. Hasn't fear taken enough? Enough smiles? Chuckles? Restful nights, exuberant days? Meet your fears with faith.

Do what my father urged my brother and me to do. Summertime for the Lucado family always involved a trip from West Texas to the Rocky Mountains. My dad loved to fish for trout on the edge of the white water rivers. Yet he knew that the currents were dangerous and his sons could be careless. Upon arrival we'd scout out the safe places to cross the river. He'd walk us down the bank until we found a line of stable rocks. He was even known to add one or two to compensate for our short strides.

As we watched, he'd test the stones, knowing if they held him, they'd hold us. Once he was on the other side, he'd signal for us to follow.

"Don't be afraid," he could have said. "Trust me."

We children never needed coaxing. But we adults often do. Does a river of fear run between you and Jesus? Cross over to him. Had Jairus waved Jesus away, death would have taken his hope. If you wave Jesus away, joy will die, laughter will perish, and tomorrow will be buried in today's grave of dread.

Don't make that mistake. Give the day a chance. Believe he can. Believe he cares. Believe he comes. Don't be afraid. Just believe.

GRACE MATTERS

On a splendid April afternoon in 2008, two college women's softball teams—one from Oregon, one from Washington—squared off beneath the blue sky of the Cascade Mountains. Inside a chainlink fence before a hundred fans, the two teams played a decisive game. The winner would advance to the division playoffs. The loser would hang up the gloves and go home.

The Western Oregon Wolves were a sturdy team that boasted several strong batters, but Sara Tucholsky was not one of them. She hit .153 and played in the game only because the first-string right fielder had muffed a play earlier in the day. Sara had never hit a home run, but on that Saturday, with two runners on base, she connected with a curveball and sent it sailing over the left-field fence.

In her excitement Sara missed first base. Her coach shouted for her to return and touch it. When she turned and started back, something popped in her knee, and down she went. She dragged herself back to the bag, pulled her knee to her chest in pain, and asked the first-base coach, "What do I do?"

The umpire wasn't sure. He knew if any of Sara's teammates assisted her, she would be out. Sara knew if she tried to stand, she would collapse. Her team couldn't help her. Her leg couldn't support her. How could she cross home plate? The umpires huddled to talk.[1]

And while they huddle and Sara groans, may I make a comparison? Blame it on the preacher in me, but I see an illustration in this moment. You and I have a lot in common with Sara Tucholsky. We, too, have stumbled. Not in baseball, but in life. In morality, honesty, integrity. We have done our best, only to trip and fall. Our finest efforts have left us flat on our backs. Like Sara, we are weakened, not with torn ligaments, but with broken hearts, weary spirits, and fading vision. The distance between where we are and where we want to be is impassable. What do we do? Where do we turn?

I suggest we turn to one of the sweetest promises:

> For our high priest [Jesus] is able to understand our weaknesses. He was tempted in every way that we are, but he did not sin. Let us, then, feel very sure that we can come before God's throne where there is grace. There we can receive mercy and grace to help us when we need it. (Heb. 4:15–16 NCV)

We have a high priest who is able to understand. Since he understands, we find mercy and grace when we need it. We are not left to languish. When we fall, we are not forgotten. When we stumble, we aren't abandoned. Our God gets us.

Theology textbooks discuss this promise under the heading "Incarnation." The stunning idea is simply this: God, for a time, became one of us. "The Word became flesh and made his dwelling among us. We have seen his glory, the glory of the one and only Son, who came from the Father, full of grace and truth" (John 1:14).

God became flesh in the form of Jesus Christ. He was miraculously conceived, yet naturally delivered. He was born, yet born of a virgin.

Had Jesus simply descended to earth in the form of a mighty being, we would respect him but never would draw near to him. After all, how could God understand what it means to be human?

Had Jesus been biologically conceived with two earthly parents, we would draw near to him, but would we want to worship him? After all, he would be no different than you and me.

But if Jesus was both—God and man at the same time—then we have the best of both worlds. Neither his humanity nor deity compromised. He was fully human. He was fully divine. Because of the first, we draw near. Because of the latter, we worship.

Such is the message of Colossians 1:15–16.

> The Son is the image of the invisible God, the firstborn over all creation. For in him all things were created: things in heaven and on earth, visible and invisible, whether thrones or powers or rulers or authorities; all things have been created through him and for him.

Not one drop of divinity was lost in the change to humanity. Though Jesus appeared human, he was actually God. The fullness of God, every bit of him, took residence in the body of Christ. "It was the Father's good pleasure for all the fullness to dwell in

Him" (Col. 1:19 NASB). The star maker, for a time, built cabinets in Nazareth.

Jesus may have looked human, but those nearest him knew he was prone to divine exclamations. Every so often Jesus let his divinity take over. The bystanders had no option but to step back and ask, "What kind of man is this? Even the winds and the waves obey him!" (Matt. 8:27).

Some years ago I served as the teacher at a weeklong Bible retreat. There is much to recall about the event. The food was phenomenal. The seaside setting was spectacular. I made several new friends. Yet, of all the memories, the one I will never forget is the Friday night basketball game.

The idea was hatched the moment David arrived. The attendees did not know he was coming, but as soon as he walked into the room, they knew who he was: David Robinson. NBA All-Star. MVP. Three-time Olympian. Two-time gold medal winner. Dream Team member. Two-time NBA champion. College All-American. Seven feet and one inch of raw talent. Body, ripped. Skills, honed. Basketball IQ, legendary.

By the end of the first day, someone asked me, "Any chance he would play basketball with us?" "Us" was a collection of pudgy, middle-aged, well-meaning but out-of-shape fellows. Bodies, plump. Skills, pathetic. Basketball IQ, slightly less than that of a squirrel.

Still, I asked David. And David, in a display of utter indulgence, said yes.

We scheduled the game, *the game*, for Friday night, the last night of the seminar. Attendance in the Bible classes declined.

Attendance on the basketball court increased. Fellows who hadn't dribbled a ball since middle school could be seen heaving shot after shot at the basket. The net was seldom threatened.

The night of the game, *the game*, David walked onto the court for the first time all week. As he warmed up, the rest of us stopped. The ball fit in his hand like a tennis ball would in mine. He carried on conversations while dribbling the ball, spinning the ball on a finger, and passing the ball behind his back. When the game began, it was David and we children. He held back. We could tell. Even so, he still took one stride for our two. He caught the ball with one hand instead of two. When he threw the ball, it was more a missile than a pass. He played basketball at a level we could only dream about.

At one point—just for the fun of it, I suppose—he let loose. The same guy who had slam-dunked basketballs over Michael Jordan and Charles Barkley let it go. I suppose he just couldn't hold it back any longer. With three strides he roared from half court to the rim. The pudgy, middle-aged opposition cleared a path as he sailed, head level with the basket, and slammed the ball with a force that left the backboard shaking.

We gulped.

David smiled.

We got the message. That's how the game is meant to be played. We may have shared the same court, but we didn't share the same power.

I'm thinking the followers of Jesus might have had a similar thought. On the day Jesus commanded the demons to leave the possessed man and they did. On the day Jesus told the storm to be quiet and it was. On the days Jesus told the dead man to rise up, the dead daughter to sit up, the entombed Lazarus to come out, and he did, she did, and he did.

"God was pleased for all of himself to live in Christ" (Col. 1:19 NCV). Jesus was undiluted deity.

No wonder no one argued when he declared, "All authority in heaven and on earth has been given to me" (Matt. 28:18).

You think the moon affects the tides? It does. But Christ runs the moon. You think the United States is a superpower? The United States has only the power Christ gives and nothing more. He has authority over everything. And he has had it forever.

Yet, in spite of this lofty position, Jesus was willing for a time to forgo the privileges of divinity and enter humanity.

He was born just as all babies are born. His childhood was a common one. "Jesus grew in wisdom and stature, and in favor with God and man" (Luke 2:52). His body developed. His muscles strengthened. His bones matured. There is no evidence or suggestion that he was spared the inconveniences of adolescence. He may have been gangly or homely. He knew the pain of sore muscles and the sting of salt in an open wound. As an adult he was weary enough to sit down at a well (John 4:6) and sleepy enough to doze off in a rocking boat (Mark 4:35–38). He became hungry in the wilderness and thirsty on the cross. When the soldiers pounded the nails through his skin, a thousand nerve endings cried for relief. As he hung limp on the cross, two human lungs begged for oxygen.

The Word became flesh.

Does this promise matter? If you ever wonder if God understands you, it does. If you ever wonder if God listens, it does. If you ever wonder if the Uncreated Creator can, in a million years, comprehend the challenges you face, then ponder long and hard the promise of the incarnation. Jesus is "able to understand our weaknesses" (Heb. 4:15 NCV). The One who hears your prayers understands your pain. He never shrugs or scoffs or dismisses physical struggle. He had a human body.

Are you troubled in spirit? He was too (John 12:27).
Are you so anxious you could die? He was too (Matt. 26:38).
Are you overwhelmed with grief? He was too (John 11:35).
Have you ever prayed with loud cries and tears? He did too
     (Heb. 5:7).

He gets you.

So human he could touch his people. So mighty he could heal them. So human he spoke with an accent. So heavenly he spoke with authority. So human he could blend in unnoticed for thirty years. So mighty he could change history and be unforgotten for two thousand years. All man. Yet all God.

I once waded into the Jordan River. On a trip to Israel my family and I stopped to see the traditional spot of Jesus' baptism. It's a charming place. Sycamores cast their shadows. Birds chirp. The water invites. So I accepted the invitation and waded in to be baptized.

No one wanted to join me, so I immersed myself. I declared my belief in Christ and sank so low in the water I could touch the river bottom. When I did, I felt a stick and pulled it out. A baptism memento! Some people get certificates or Bibles; I like my stick. It's about as thick as your wrist, long as your forearm, and smooth as a baby's behind. I keep it on my office credenza so I can show it to fear-filled people.

When they chronicle their anxieties about the economy or their concerns about their kids, I hand them the stick. I tell them how God muddied his feet in our world of diapers, death, digestion, and disease. How John the Baptist told him to stay on the riverbank but Jesus wouldn't listen. How he came to earth for this very purpose—to become one of us. "Why, he might have touched this very stick," I like to say.

As they smile, I ask, "Since he came this far to reach us, can't we take our fears to him?" Read the promise again, slowly, thoughtfully.

For our high priest [Jesus] is able to understand our weaknesses. He was tempted in every way that we are, but he did not sin. Let us, then, feel very sure that we can come before God's throne where there is grace. There we can receive mercy and grace to help us when we need it. (Heb. 4:15–16 NCV)

Some have pointed to the sinlessness of Jesus as evidence that he cannot fully understand us. If he never sinned, they reason, how could he understand the full force of sin? Simple. He felt it more than we do. We give in! He never did. We surrender. He never did. He stood before the tsunami of temptation and never wavered. In that manner he understands it more than anyone who ever lived.

And then, in his grandest deed, he volunteered to feel the consequences of sin. "God made him who had no sin to be sin for us, so that in him we might become the righteousness of God" (2 Cor. 5:21).

Jesus didn't deserve to feel the shame, but he felt it. He didn't deserve the humiliation, but he experienced it. He had never sinned, yet he was treated like a sinner. He became sin. All the guilt, remorse, and embarrassment—Jesus understands it.

Does this promise matter? To the hypocrite, it does. To the person with the hangover and fuzzy memory about last night's party, it does. To the cheater, slanderer, gossip, or scoundrel who comes to God with a humble spirit, it matters. It matters because they need to know that we can "approach God's throne of grace with confidence, so that we may receive mercy and find grace to help us in our time of need" (Heb. 4:16).

Because Jesus is human, he understands you.

Because he is divine, he can help you.

He is uniquely positioned to carry us home. Jesus does for us what Mallory Holtman did for Sara Tucholsky. Sara, remember, is the girl who tore an ACL during her home-run trot. When we left her, she was lying on the ground, clutching her knee with one hand and touching first base with the other. The umpires huddled. The players stood and watched. The fans shouted for someone to take Sara off the field, but she didn't want to leave. She wanted to cross home plate.

Mallory Holtman came up with a solution.

She played first base for the opposing team, Central Washington University. She was a senior and wanted a victory. A loss would end her season. You'd think Mallory would be happy to see the home run nullified. She wasn't.

"Hey," she said to the umpires. "Can I help her around the bases?"

"Why would you want to do that?" one asked. Before she could answer, the ump shrugged and said, "Do it."

So Mallory did. She signaled for the shortstop to help her, and the two walked toward the injured player. "We're going to pick you up and carry you around the bases."

By this time tears streaked Sara's cheeks. "Thank you."

Mallory and her friend put one hand under Sara's legs and the other hand under Sara's arms. The mission of mercy began. They paused long enough at second and third base to lower Sara's foot to touch the bases. By the time they headed home, the spectators had risen to their feet, Sara's teammates had gathered at home plate, and Sara was smiling like a homecoming queen.[2]

Well she should. The only one who could help did help. And because she did, Sara made it home.

God offers to do the same for you and me. Mallory's message for Sara is God's message for us: "I'm going to pick you up and carry you home." Let him, won't you? You cannot make it on your own. But Jesus has the strength you do not have. He is, after all, your high priest, able and willing to help in your time of need.

Let him do what he came to do. Let him carry you home.

SALVATION

Are you really *saved*? Many people don't know. Many Christians don't know. They live with a deep-seated anxiety about eternity. They think they are saved, hope they are saved, but still they doubt.

It seeps into the thoughts of the dying. When we forget our vow to God, does God forget us? Does God place us on a standby list?

Our behavior gives us reason to wonder. We are strong one day, weak the next. Devoted one hour, flagging the next. Believing, then unbelieving. Our lives mirror the contours of a roller coaster—highs and lows.

Conventional wisdom draws a line through the middle of these fluctuations. Perform above this line, and enjoy God's acceptance. But dip below it, and expect a pink slip from heaven. In this paradigm a person is lost and saved multiple times a day, in and out of the kingdom on a regular basis. Salvation becomes a matter of timing. You just hope you die on an upswing. No security, stability, or confidence.

This is not God's plan. He draws the line, for sure. But he draws it beneath our ups and downs. Jesus' language couldn't be stronger: "And I give them eternal life, and they shall never lose it or perish throughout the ages. [To all eternity they shall never by any means be destroyed.] And no one is able to snatch them out of My hand" (John 10:28 AMPC).

Jesus promised a new life that could not be forfeited or terminated. "Whoever hears my word and believes him who sent me has eternal life and will not be judged but has crossed over from death to life" (John 5:24). Bridges are burned, and the transfer is accomplished. Ebbs and flows continue, but they never disqualify. Ups and downs may mark our days, but they will never ban us from his kingdom. Jesus bottom lines our lives with grace.

Even more, God stakes his claim on us. "By his Spirit he has stamped us with his eternal pledge—a sure beginning of what he is destined to complete" (2 Cor. 1:22 THE MESSAGE). You've done something similar: engraved your name on a piece of jewelry, etched your identity on a tool, or monogrammed a gift. Cowboys brand cattle with the mark of the ranch. Stamping declares ownership. Through his Spirit, God stamps us. Would-be takers are repelled by the presence of his name. Satan is driven back by the declaration: *Hands off. This child is mine! Eternally, God.*

On-and-off salvation never appears in the Bible. Salvation is not a repeated phenomenon. Scripture contains no example of a person who was saved, then lost, then resaved, then lost again.

Where there is no assurance of salvation, there is no peace. No peace means no joy. No joy results in fear-based lives. Is this the life God creates? No. Grace creates a confident soul who declares, "I know whom I have believed, and am convinced that he is able to guard what I have entrusted to him until that day" (2 Tim. 1:12).

Of all we don't know in life, we know this: we hold a boarding pass. "These things I have written to you who believe in the name of the Son of God, that you may know that you have eternal life" (1 John 5:13 NKJV). Trust God's hold on you more than your hold on God. His faithfulness does not depend on yours. His performance is not predicated on yours. His love is not contingent on your own. Your candle may flicker, but it will not expire.

Do you find such a promise hard to believe? The disciples did. On the night before his death, Jesus made this announcement: "All of you will be made to stumble because of Me this night, for it is written: 'I will strike the Shepherd, and the sheep of the flock will be scattered.' But after I have been raised, I will go before you to Galilee" (Matt. 26:31–32 NKJV).

By this point the disciples had known Jesus for three years. They'd spent a thousand nights with him. They knew his stride, accent, and sense of humor. They'd smelled his breath, heard him snore, and watched him pick his teeth after dinner. They'd witnessed miracles we know about and countless more we don't. Bread multiplied. Lepers cleansed. They saw him turn water into Chablis and a lunch box into a buffet. They unwrapped burial clothing from a was-dead Lazarus. They watched mud fall from the eyes of a was-blind man. For three years these handpicked recruits enjoyed front-row, center-court seats to heaven's greatest display. And how would they respond?

"All of you will stumble," Jesus told them. Fall away. Turn away. Run away. Their promises would melt like wax on a summer sidewalk. Jesus' promise, however, would stay firm. "But after I have been raised, I will go before you to Galilee" (v. 32). Translation? Your fall will be great, but my grace will be greater. Stumble, I will catch you. Scatter, I will gather you. Turn from me, I will turn toward you. You'll find me waiting for you in Galilee.

The promise was lost on Peter. "Even if all are made to stumble because of You, I will never be made to stumble" (v. 33 NKJV).

Not one of Peter's finer moments. "Even if all . . ." Arrogant. "I will never be made to stumble." Self-sufficient. Peter's trust was in Peter's strength. Yet Peter's strength would peter out. Jesus knew it: "Simon, Simon! Indeed, Satan has asked for you, that he may sift you as wheat. But I have prayed for you, that your faith should not fail; and when you have returned to Me, strengthen your brethren" (Luke 22:31–32 NKJV).

Satan would attack and test Peter. But Satan would never claim

Peter. Why? Because Peter was strong? No, because Jesus was. "I have prayed for you." Jesus' prayers hamstring Satan.

Jesus prays for you as well: "Holy Father . . . now protect them by the power of your name so that they will be united just as we are. . . . I am praying not only for these disciples but also for all who will ever believe in me through their message" (John 17:11, 20 NLT).

Will God hear the intercessory pleas of his Son? Of course he will. Like Peter, we may be sifted like wheat. Our faith will wane, our resolve waver, but we will not fall away. We are "kept safe by Jesus Christ" (Jude v. 1 THE MESSAGE) and "shielded by God's power" (1 Peter 1:5). And that is no small power. It is the power of a living and ever-persistent Savior.

But might some take advantage of this assurance? Knowing that God will catch them if they fall, might they fall on purpose? Yes, they might, for a time. But as grace goes deep, as God's love and kindness sink in, they will change. Grace fosters obedience.

Look to Christ for your beginning and ending. He is the Alpha and Omega. He will hold you. And he will hold on to the ones you love. Do you have a prodigal? Do you long for your spouse to return to God? Do you have a friend whose faith has grown cold? God wants them back more than you do. Keep praying, but don't give up.

God places a song in the hearts of his children. A song of hope and life. "He has put a new song in my mouth" (Ps. 40:3 NKJV). Some saints sing this song loud and long every single day of their lives. In other cases the song falls silent. Life's hurts and happenings mute the music within. Long seasons pass in which God's song is not sung.

I want to be careful here. Truth is, we do not always know if someone has trusted God's grace. A person may have feigned belief but not meant it.[3] It isn't ours to know. But we know this: where there is genuine conversion, there is eternal salvation. Our task is to trust God's ability to call his children home. We join God as he walks among his wayward and wounded children, singing.

Eventually his own will hear his voice, and something within them will awaken. And when it does, they will begin to sing again.

QUESTIONS FOR REFLECTION

1. Back in the bustling seaside city of Capernaum, we meet Jairus, a city official whose daughter is dying. Jesus promised to help him but was distracted by a woman who touched his cloak, and Jairus, desperate for his daughter to be healed, began to wonder if Jesus would make good on his promise.

   • When you're in need, what is hardest to believe about Jesus: that he can, that he cares, or that he'll come?

   • How did Jesus show Jairus that he could, that he cared, and that he would come? (Mark 5:40–41)

   • What does this tell you about how Jesus will answer your prayers?

2. In need of strength? In hope of a miracle? Max urges us to recall "one of the sweetest promises" of Scripture: Hebrews 4:15–16.

- What does this promise mean to you?
- Remember a time you held on to this promise. What challenge were you facing? How did recalling the promise make a difference?
- "The one who hears your prayers understands your pain." Have you experienced the truth of this claim? How did it recalibrate your faith?

3. Jesus promised eternity to those who trust their souls to him. "Whoever hears my word and believes him who sent me has eternal life" (John 5:24).
   - Where do you turn when life turns dark? Do you find it natural to seek God's voice in your pain?
   - When you imagine Jesus, how do you picture him? The sleepy Savior in a storm-rocked boat? The confident healer at a dead girl's bedside? The teacher speaking to thousands on a Palestine hillside? What image comforts you? Why?
   - "The One who hears your prayers understands your pain." Why do you know this is true?

4. Max said, "Trust God's hold on you more than your hold on God. His faithfulness does not depend on yours. His performance is not predicated on yours. His love is not contingent on your own" (p. 105).
   - How do you feel about these statements?
   - Do you find them difficult or easy to believe? Why?

Psephinus Tower*

Tyropoeon Street***

Present Damascus Gate***

Bridge Over Valley*** ("Wilson's Arch")

Xystus (Greek exercise hall)*

Hasmonean Palace*

Traditional Crucifixion Site †††

Herod's Towers

Herod's Royal Palace*

t. Zion Jpper City")

heater**

Traditional Upper Room?

Essene Gate

House of Caiaphas

HINNOM VALLEY

Ashpot Gate (Tekoa Gate)

Pool of Siloam***

City of David ("Lower City")

KIDRON VALLEY

Gihon Spring***

Huldah Gates and Stairways***

Gentiles Court

Temple

Pool of Bethesda***

Bezetha ("New City")

Antonia Fortress*** (later Praetorium?)

"Garden Tomb" (alternate crucifixion site) †††

Maximum city growth within walls by AD 70

Hippo

N

MOUNT OF OLIVES

PART 3

THE CROSSROADS AND THE CROSS

Jerusalem

Tradition points to the "Garden Tomb" as a possible location for Jesus' tomb. It was here Jesus made his final declaration: he'd rather die for you than live without you. This place of death and sadness became the ultimate symbol of life and our eternal hope. The apostle Paul wrote these cherished words: "Death has been swallowed up in victory." The Christian promise is this: You give Christ your life; he takes care of your death. He makes sure that you get home safely. The fact of his resurrection is the promise of yours.

CHAPTER 8

FACING DOUBTERS, DENIERS, AND DEFENDERS

To understand John 3:16—indeed to understand Jesus—this title is required reading: ". . . one and only Son. . . ."

"For God so loved the world that he gave his one and only Son, that whoever believes in him shall not perish but have eternal life" (John 3:16).

Jesus, the one and only.

The Greek word for "one and only" is *monogenes*, an adjective compounded of *monos*—"only" and *genes*—"species, race, family, offspring, kind." When used in the Bible, it almost always describes a parent-child relationship. Luke uses it to describe the widow's son: "the only son of his mother" (Luke 7:12). The writer of Hebrews states: "Abraham . . . was ready to sacrifice his only son, Isaac" (Heb. 11:17 NLT).

John employs the term five times, in each case highlighting the unparalleled relationship between Jesus and God.

> The Word became flesh and made his dwelling among us. We have seen his glory, the glory of the one and only Son, who came from the Father, full of grace and truth. (John 1:14)

> No one has ever seen God, but the one and only Son, who is himself God and is in closest relationship with the Father, has made him known. (John 1:18)

> For God so loved the world that he gave his one and only Son, that whoever believes in him shall not perish but have eternal life. (John 3:16)

> Whoever believes in him is not condemned, but whoever does not believe stands condemned already because they have not believed in the name of God's one and only Son. (John 3:18)

> This is how God showed his love among us: He sent his one and only Son into the world that we might live through him. (1 John 4:9)

In all five appearances the adjective modifies the subject "Son."

Bethlehem today

Fields just outside Bethlehem where shepherds watched over their flocks

Modern-day Nazareth as seen from the top of Mount Precipice

Wadi Qelt in the Judean wilderness with a winding path from Jericho to Jerusalem

Springtime view of the Sea of Galilee from the Mount of Beatitudes

Olive trees in the garden of Gethsemane where Jesus prayed

Max teaching by the Sea of Galilee

Traditional location of the upper room where the Last Supper was held

Fourth-century synagogue built on top of first-century ruins, Capernaum

Darker basalt rocks are the first-century foundations of synagogue ruins in Capernaum

The "streets of gold" in the Old City of Jerusalem

The Via Dolorosa—the Way of Suffering, in the Old City of Jerusalem

Palm Sunday road leading into the Old City of Jerusalem from the Mount of Olives

Max teaching at the Garden Tomb

The Garden Tomb

Inside the Garden Tomb

The road to Emmaus where Jesus appeared to his disciples after his resurrection

A rainbow over the Old City of Jerusalem—a reminder of God's covenant with Noah

"Monogenes," then, highlights the singular relationship between Jesus and God. He is a Son in a sense that no one else is. All who call on him are children of God, but Jesus alone is the Son of God. Only Christ is called "monogenes," because only Christ has God's genes or genetic makeup.

The familiar translation "only begotten Son" (John 3:16 NKJV) conveys this truth. When parents "beget" or conceive a child, they transfer their DNA to the newborn. Jesus shares God's DNA. He isn't begotten in the sense that he began but in the sense that he and God have the same essence, same eternal essence, unending wisdom, tireless energy. Every quality you give God, you can give Jesus. Jesus claimed: "Anyone who has seen me has seen the Father!" (John 14:9 NLT).

And the epistle concurred: "This Son perfectly mirrors God, and is stamped with God's nature" (Heb. 1:3 THE MESSAGE).

Jesus enjoys a relationship with God that is unknown and unexperienced by anyone else in history; he claims to occupy the Christ the Redeemer perch. Through the pen of Matthew he gives two features of the relationship.

> My Father has entrusted everything to me. No one truly knows the Son except the Father, and no one truly knows the Father except the Son and those to whom the Son chooses to reveal him. (Matt. 11:27 NLT)

Via these words he calls himself the One and Only Ruler. "My Father has entrusted everything to me" (Matt. 11:27 NLT). With that holy authority came power. Power to condemn, power to forgive, and the wisdom and discernment necessary for both. The Son understood this responsibility. Never more so than one day at the temple . . .

The voices had yanked her out of bed.

"Get up, you harlot."

"What kind of woman do you think you are?"

Priests had slammed open the bedroom door, thrown back the window curtains, and pulled off the covers. Before she felt the warmth of the morning sun, she had felt the heat of their scorn.

"Shame on you."

"Pathetic."

"Disgusting."

She scarcely had time to cover her body before they marched her through the narrow streets. Dogs yelped. Roosters ran. Women leaned out their windows. Mothers snatched children off the path. Merchants peered out the doors of their shops. Jerusalem became a jury and rendered its verdict with glares and crossed arms.

And as if the bedroom raid and parade of shame were inadequate, the men thrust her into the middle of a morning Bible class.

Early the next morning [Jesus] was back again at the Temple. A crowd soon gathered, and he sat down and taught them. As he was speaking, the teachers of religious law and the Pharisees brought a woman who had been caught in the act of adultery. They put her in front of the crowd.

"Teacher," they said to Jesus, "this woman was caught in the act of adultery. The law of Moses says to stone her. What do you say?" (John 8:2–5 NLT)

Stunned students stood on one side of her. Pious plaintiffs on the other. They had their questions and convictions; she had her dangling negligee and smeared lipstick. "This woman was caught in the act of adultery," her accusers crowed. Caught in the very act. In the moment. In the arms. In the passion. Caught in the act by the Jerusalem Council on Decency and Conduct. "The law of Moses says to stone her. What do you say?"

The woman had no exit. Deny the accusation? She had been caught. Plead for mercy? From whom? From God? His spokesmen were squeezing stones and snarling their lips. No one would speak for her.

But someone would stoop for her.

"Jesus stooped down and wrote in the dust" (v. 6 NLT). We would expect him to stand up, step forward, or even ascend a stair and speak. But instead he leaned over. He descended lower than anyone else—beneath the priests and the people and even beneath the woman. The accusers looked down on her. To see Jesus, they had to look down even farther.

He's prone to stoop. He stooped to wash feet, to embrace children. Stooped to pull Peter out of the sea, to pray in the garden. He stooped before the Roman whipping post. Stooped to carry the cross. Grace is a God who stoops. Here he stooped to write in the dust.

Remember the first occasion his fingers touched dirt? He scooped soil and formed Adam. As he touched the sunbaked soil beside the woman, Jesus may have been reliving the Creation moment, reminding himself from whence we came. Earthly humans are prone to do earthy things. Maybe Jesus wrote in the soil for his own benefit.

Or for hers? To divert gaping eyes from the scantily clad, just-caught woman who stood in the center of the circle?

The posse grew impatient with the silent, stooping Jesus. "They kept demanding an answer, so he stood up" (v. 7 NLT).

He lifted himself erect until his shoulders were straight and his head was high. He stood, not to preach, for his words would be few. Not for long, for he would soon stoop again. Not to instruct his followers; he didn't address them. He stood on behalf of the woman. He placed himself between her and the lynch mob and said, "'All right, but let the one who has never sinned throw the first stone!' Then he stooped down again and wrote in the dust" (vv. 7–8 NLT).

Name-callers shut their mouths. Rocks fell to the ground. Jesus resumed his scribbling. "When the accusers heard this, they slipped away one by one, beginning with the oldest, until only Jesus was left in the middle of the crowd with the woman" (v. 9 NLT).

Jesus wasn't finished. He stood one final time and asked the woman, "Where are your accusers?" (v. 10 NLT).

My, my, my. What a question—not just for her but for us. Voices of condemnation awaken us as well.

"You aren't good enough."

"You'll never improve."

"You failed—again."

The voices in our world.

And the voices in our heads! Who is this morality patrolman who issues a citation at every stumble? Who reminds us of every mistake? Does he ever shut up?

No. Because Satan never shuts up. The apostle John called him the accuser: "This great dragon—the ancient serpent called the devil, or Satan, the one deceiving the whole world—was thrown down to the earth with all his angels. Then I heard a loud voice shouting across the heavens, '. . . For the accuser of our brothers and sisters has been thrown down to earth—the one who accuses them before our God day and night'" (Rev. 12:9–10 NLT).

Day after day, hour after hour. Relentless, tireless. The accuser makes a career out of accusing. Unlike the conviction of the Holy Spirit, Satan's condemnation brings no repentance or resolve, just regret. He has one aim: "to steal and kill and destroy" (John 10:10 NLT). Steal your peace, kill your dreams, and destroy your future. He has deputized a horde of silver-tongued demons to help him. He enlists people to peddle his poison. Friends dredge up your past. Preachers proclaim all guilt and no grace. And parents, oh, your parents. They own a travel agency that specializes in guilt trips. They distribute it twenty-four hours a day. Long into adulthood you still hear their voices: "Why can't you grow up?" "When are you going to make me proud?"

Condemnation—the preferred commodity of Satan. He will repeat the adulterous woman scenario as often as you permit him to do so, marching you through the city streets and dragging your name through the mud. He pushes you into the center of the crowd and megaphones your sin: This person was caught in the act of immorality . . . stupidity . . . dishonesty . . . irresponsibility.

But he will not have the last word. Jesus has acted on your behalf.

He stooped. Low enough to sleep in a manger, work in a

carpentry shop, sleep in a fishing boat. Low enough to rub shoulders with crooks and lepers. Low enough to be spat upon, slapped, nailed, and speared. Low. Low enough to be buried.

And then he stood. Up from the slab of death. Upright in the tomb and right in Satan's face. Tall. High. He stood up for the woman and silenced her accusers, and he does the same for you.

He "is in the presence of God at this very moment sticking up for us" (Rom. 8:34 THE MESSAGE). Let this sink in for a moment. In the presence of God, in defiance of Satan, Jesus Christ rises to your defense. He takes on the role of a priest. "Since we have a great priest over God's house, let us come near to God with a sincere heart and a sure faith, because we have been made free from a guilty conscience" (Heb. 10:21–22 NCV).

A clean conscience. A clean record. A clean heart. Free from accusation. Free from condemnation. Not just for our past mistakes but also for our future ones. "Since he will live forever, he will always be there to remind God that he has paid for [our] sins with his blood" (Heb. 7:25 TLB). Christ offers unending intercession on your behalf.

Jesus trumps the devil's guilt with words of grace.

Though we were spiritually dead because of the things we did against God, he gave us new life with Christ. You have been saved by God's grace. And he raised us up with Christ and gave us a seat with him in the heavens. He did this for those in Christ Jesus so that for all future time he could show the very great riches of his grace by being kind to us in Christ Jesus. I mean that you have been saved by grace through believing. You did not save yourselves; it was a gift from God. It was not the result of your own efforts, so you cannot brag about it. God has made us what we are. In Christ Jesus, God made us to do good works, which God planned in advance for us to live our lives doing. (Eph. 2:5–10 NCV)

Behold the fruit of grace: saved by God, raised by God, seated with God. Gifted, equipped, and commissioned. Farewell, earthly condemnations: Stupid. Unproductive. Slow learner. Fast talker. Quitter. Cheapskate. No longer. You are who he says you are: Spiritually alive. Heavenly positioned. Connected to God. A billboard of mercy. An honored child. This is the "aggressive forgiveness we call *grace*" (Rom. 5:20 THE MESSAGE).

Satan is left speechless and without ammunition.

Who can accuse the people God has chosen? No one, because God is the One who makes them right. Who can say God's people are guilty? No one, because Christ Jesus died, but he was also raised from the dead, and now he is on God's right side, appealing to God for us. (Rom. 8:33–34 NCV)

The accusations of Satan sputter and fall like a deflated balloon.

Then why, pray tell, do we still hear them? Why do we, as Christians, still feel guilt?

Not all guilt is bad. God uses appropriate doses of guilt to awaken us to sin. We know guilt is God-given when it causes "indignation . . . alarm . . . longing . . . concern . . . readiness to see justice done" (2 Cor. 7:11). God's guilt brings enough regret to change us.

Satan's guilt, on the other hand, brings enough regret to enslave us. Don't let him lock his shackles on you.

Remember, "your life is hidden with Christ in God" (Col. 3:3 NKJV). When he looks at you, he sees Jesus first. In the Chinese language the word for righteousness is a combination of two characters: the figure of a lamb and a person. The lamb is on top, covering the person. Whenever God looks down at you, this is what he sees: the perfect Lamb of God covering you. It boils down to this choice: Do you trust your Advocate or your accuser?

Your answer has serious implications.

Grace changes people. Let it change you. Give no heed to Satan's voice. You "have an Advocate with the Father, Jesus Christ the righteous" (1 John 2:1 NKJV). As your Advocate, he defends you and says on your behalf, "There is therefore now no condemnation to those who are in Christ Jesus" (Rom. 8:1 NKJV). Take that, Satan!

Wasn't this the message of Jesus to the woman?

"Where are your accusers? Didn't even one of them condemn you?"

"No, Lord," she said.

And Jesus said, "Neither do I. Go and sin no more." (John 8:10–11 NLT)

Within a few moments the courtyard was empty. Jesus, the woman, her critics—they all left. But let's linger. Look at the rocks on the ground, abandoned and unused. And look at the scribbling in the dust. It's the only sermon Jesus ever wrote. Even though we don't know the words, I'm wondering if they read like this: *Grace happens here.*

QUESTIONS FOR REFLECTION

1. What does the Greek word *monogenes* mean? How can this definition help us understand the phrase "one and only" when used to describe Jesus, the Son?
   - What is the Son's relationship to the Father?
   - How is their relationship different from an earthly father and his son?

2. How is Jesus our one and only ruler?
   - Which Jesus do you need today?
     - The ruler who is the ultimate authority in your life?
     - The one whose ways are higher than your ways?
     - Or the one who knows the Father more intimately than anyone else?
   - Why?

3. In Jerusalem as Jesus was teaching a group of men in the temple, a woman was brought before him who had been "caught in the act of adultery" (John 8:4). The Pharisees were calling for her death.

- What hope did this woman have, shamed by the group of men around her, hearing her death sentence publicly announced?
- How did Jesus' presence change the situation and bring hope for the woman?
- What is something you feel shame about in your life?
- How could this story bring you hope in this shame?

4. Read Matthew 11:28–29.
   - What is Jesus teaching you right now?
   - What do you need him to teach you?

5. What reasons did Max offer that could explain why Jesus stooped to write in the dirt when the woman was brought to him?
   - Why do you think Jesus began to write in the dirt?
   - What do you think he wrote?
   - Considering what you just learned about Jesus' relationship to the Father, why is it significant that he would stoop in the presence of the woman caught in adultery?
   - What do you think the men who gathered at the Temple thought of Jesus' behavior?
   - What do you think of his behavior?

6. What does the voice of your accuser sound like?
   - What does this voice tell you?

- How does this voice affect you in your work, relationships with others, and relationship with God?
- Read Romans 8:33–34. Why can no one accuse you or call you guilty?
- Silence the voice of your accuser and spend a few moments listening for the voice of Jesus, your Advocate. What is he telling you?

CHAPTER 9

SPEAKING ETERNAL TRUTH TO EARTHLY POWERS

Several years ago I received an urgent call to visit a dying man in the hospital. I didn't know Peter well, but I knew him well enough to know he was paying a high price for his hard living. Years of drugs and alcohol abuse had perforated his system. Though he'd made peace with God through Christ, his liver was in conflict with his body.

When his ex-wife phoned me, she was standing at his bedside. Peter, she explained, was knocking at death's door. Though I hurried, he entered it minutes before I arrived. The hospital room had a "just happened" feel to it. She was still standing by the bed. His hair was stroked back from her touch. The imprint of a lipstick kiss was just below the knuckles on his left hand. Perspiration beads sparkled on his forehead.

She saw me enter and looked up. With eyes and words, she explained, "He just left."

Peter silently slipped out. Exited. Departed. One moment here. The next moment . . . where? He passed, not away, but on. Yet on to where? And in what form? To what place? In what manner? And, once there, what did he see? Know or do? We so desire to know.

Who in your life "just left"? When the breathing of your spouse ceased, the beating heart in your womb stopped, or the beep of your grandmother's monitor became a flat-lined tone, what happened in that moment?

And what will happen to you in yours? Barring the return of Christ, you will have one . . . a last gasp, a final pulse. Your lungs will empty and blood will still. And . . . then what? What will we be after we die? What will happen after we die? Answers vary.

- Nothing, some people say. We will decay and/or disintegrate. Death is a dead end. Our works and reputation might survive, but not us.
- We become ghosts, perhaps? Phantoms of what we once were. Pale as a snowdrift. Structured as a morning mist. What will we be after we die? Specters?
- Or hawks, or cows, or a car mechanic in Kokomo. Reincarnation rewards or punishes us according to our behavior. We come back to earth in another mortal body.
- Or, a part of the universe. Eternity absorbs us like a lake

absorbs a raindrop. We return to what we were before we were what we are . . . we return to the cosmic consciousness of the universe.

Christianity, on the other hand, posits a new, startling idea. "Death has been swallowed up in victory" (1 Cor. 15:54). According to the promise of the empty tomb, my friend Peter awoke in a world so wondrously better than this one that it would take God himself to convince Peter to return to earth. We know this because Jesus' miracles included only three resurrections. I'm thinking he had a hard time getting return guests.

This is the Christian hope. This hope is verified by the Easter miracle. Do you know this miracle?

WHAT HAPPENED TO CHRIST?

It was Sunday morning after the Friday execution. The sky was dark. The disciples had scattered. And the Roman executioner was wondering about breakfast or work or his next day off. But he was not wondering about the fellow he had nailed to a cross and pierced with a spear. Jesus was dead and buried. Yesterday's news, right?

Wrong.

There was a violent earthquake, for an angel of the Lord came down from heaven and, going to the tomb, rolled back the stone and sat on it. His appearance was like lightning, and his clothes were white as snow. The guards were so afraid of him that they shook and became like dead men.

The angel said to the women, "Do not be afraid, for I know that you are looking for Jesus, who was crucified. He is not here; he has risen, just as he said. Come and see the place where he lay." (Matt. 28:2–6)

And out he marched, the cadaver-turned-king, with the mask of death in one hand and the keys of heaven in the other. He has risen!

Not risen from sleep. Not risen from confusion. Not risen from stupor or slumber. Not spiritually raised from the dead, physically raised. The women and disciples didn't see a phantom or experience a sentiment. They saw Jesus "in the flesh." They weren't alone. The other followers saw him. The apostles saw him. "After that He was seen by over five hundred brethren at once" (1 Cor. 15:6 NKJV).

The resurrection was no back-alley possibility. It was an actuality witnessed by hundreds of people.

We know what happened to Christ when he died. What happens to those who believe him?

WHAT HAPPENS TO CHRISTIANS?

Simple, because the tomb is empty, the promise of Christ is not. "Death has been swallowed up in victory" (1 Cor. 15:54). If you trust Christ with your life, he will take care of you in death.

When you die, your spirit will immediately enter the presence of God. You will enjoy conscious fellowship with the heavenly Father and with those who have gone before. Your body will join you later. We believe this to be true because of verses like this one: "We are confident, I say, and would prefer to be away from the body and at home with the Lord" (2 Cor. 5:8).

When Peter's ex-wife asked me what happened to him, I could rightly say, "He is away from his body and at home with the Lord."

Isn't this the promise that Jesus gave the thief on the cross? "Today you will be with me in paradise" (Luke 23:43). "Today," Christ promised. No delay. No pause. No purgatory cleansing or soul sleeping. The thief closed his eyes on earth and awoke in paradise. The soul of the believer journeys home, while the body of the believer awaits the resurrection.

Paradise is the first stage of heaven.

But paradise is not the final version of heaven. At a certain point, known today only to God, your body will someday be called from the grave. "The dead will hear the voice of the Son of God . . . all who are . . . in their graves will hear his voice . . . they will come out" (John 5:25, 28–29 NCV). A day is coming in which a new day will begin.

There is significant discussion about this moment. Does the call of Christ trigger a rapture and a tribulation? Or does it inaugurate a new kingdom and eternal reign? We will save those questions for another time when we have more time, but for today here is what we need to remember: You will do what Jesus did. You will exit your grave.

"For our citizenship is in heaven, from which we also eagerly wait for the Savior, the Lord Jesus Christ, who will transform our lowly body" (Phil. 3:20–21 NKJV).

Your body is so tired, so worn. Joints ache and muscles fatigue. Your body used to be sturdy and strong, but the days have passed, and the storms have come, and this old tent has some bare spots. The cold creeps in, and the wind makes it tilt. It's not as strong as it used to be.

Or, then again, maybe your body has never been strong. Your sight has never been crisp, your hearing has never been clear. Your walk has never been sturdy; your heart has never been steady. You've watched others take for granted the health you've never had. Wheelchairs, doctor visits, hospital rooms, needles, stethoscopes—if you never saw another one for the rest of your life, you'd be happy. You'd give anything, yes, anything, for one full day in one sure body.

If that describes you, let God speak to your heart for just a moment. You need to hear the rest of the "lowly body" verse. We only read the first half of the phrase; you'll relish the rest.

For our citizenship is in heaven, from which we also eagerly wait for the Savior, the Lord Jesus Christ, who will transform our lowly body that it may be conformed to His glorious body. (Phil. 3:20–21 NKJV)

Let's listen to another couple of versions:

He will take these dying bodies of ours and change them into glorious bodies like his own. (Phil. 3:21 TLB)

He will transfigure these wretched bodies of ours into copies of his glorious body. (Phil. 3:21 JB)

He will transfigure the body belonging to our humble state, and give it a form like that of his own resplendent body. (Phil. 3:21 NEB)

Regardless of the wording, the promise is the same. Your body will be changed.

Envision yourself as you were meant to be: completely whole.

And while your imagination is warmed up, envision this earth as it was intended to be: completely calm. "The wolf will live with the lamb, the leopard will lie down with the goat, the calf and the lion and the yearling together; and a little child will lead them" (Isa. 11:6). Lions won't snarl. Bears won't maim. No one, no thing, will rebel. The next age will be calm because it gladly defers to God.

"No longer will there be any curse" (Rev. 22:3).

No more struggle with the earth. No more shame before God. No more tension between people. No more death. No more curse. The removal of the curse will return God's people and universe to their intended state. Satan, the tempter, will be thrown "into the eternal fire prepared for the devil and his angels" (Matt. 25:41 ESV).

In that moment "Death is swallowed up in victory" (1 Cor. 15:54 NKJV). This is the hope for the Christian.

Have you made this the hope for your life?

If not, doesn't it make sense that you do so? Doesn't it make sense that you know your destination?

Travelers do. I've engaged in dozens of airplane conversations in my life. When I've asked, "Where are you headed?" people always have an answer. No one has ever said these words to me:

"I don't know, man. I'm just enjoying the journey."

Or, "Who knows. I'll just land and see where I am."

Every traveler worth a flight mile knows that the purpose of the plane is to carry us from one place to the next. Do you understand that the purpose of this life is to do the same? You were made for more than airplane peanuts and in-flight entertainment. You were made to go home.

But Christ will only receive you if you ask him.

If you've already claimed this promise, make sure you are standing on it. Make this promise one of the blocks in your foundation.

Jesus Christ rose from the dead, not just to show you his power, but to reveal your path. He will lead you through the valley of death. "Death has been swallowed up in victory" (1 Cor. 15:54).

Some time ago I spent an hour in the office of a cemetery director. Yet another birthday had reminded me that the day of my departure is increasingly near. It seemed right to me to make burial preparations. Then again, it didn't.

As the gentleman was showing me the cemetery map and the available sections, I had an idea. "You'll likely think I'm crazy," I told him, "but can I record a message for my tombstone? A sort of voice mail for the grave?"

To his credit he didn't call me crazy and promised to check. Within a few days he gave me the good news: "Yes, it is possible. A recorded message can be encased in the grave marker. At the push of the button, a message can be played."

I thanked him and got to work. Within a few minutes I had

mine written. It's not yet recorded. Perhaps I can test it with you first?

The granite stone will contain a button and an invitation: "Press for a word from Max." If you do, this is what you will hear.

> Thanks for coming by. Sorry you missed me. I'm not here. I'm home. Finally, home. At some point my King will call, and this grave will be shown for the temporary tomb it is. You might want to step to the side in case that happens while you are here. Again, I appreciate the visit. Hoping you've made plans for your own departure. All the best, Max.

Yeah, it still needs some work. While the wording might change, the promise never will: "Death has been swallowed up in victory" (1 Cor. 15:54).

SURVIVAL

Not all of you will understand the rest of this section. Not all of you will comprehend its message or relate to its promise. You won't understand it if

- you've never failed and are intolerant of those who have.
- your life is as hygienic as a new hospital and your soul could pass the white glove test.
- you are a red-hot zealot who thinks God is lucky to have you on his side.

- you dreamed of a perfect home and got it, dreamed of the perfect job and got it, dreamed of the problem-free life and got it.
- your pillow has never known tears, your prayers have never known anguish, and your faith has never known doubt.

If you are tearless and fearless and can't understand why others aren't, then this chapter is going to sound like a foreign language.

Why? Because this is a section on survival and coping with pain. The following paragraphs were not written for those on top of the world but for those trapped under one that has collapsed. If you can relate to that description, then turn to Matthew and get ready for some assurance.

That may surprise you if you know anything about Matthew 24. You remember it as the neighborhood hangout for end-times fanatics. The camping ground for eschatological mathematicians and last-days prophets.

It deserves that reputation. This section known as the Olivet discourse is Christ's proclamation of the end times. Scholars have dedicated more than one book to this one chapter to answer one question: What is Jesus saying?

Ominous phrases lurk in the chapter: "wars and threats of wars," and "how terrible it will be for pregnant women" (NLT). Eerie descriptions of the sun growing dark and the moon not giving its light. Vultures hovering around bodies and lightning flashing.

How do we explain it?

Some feel the entire chapter is symbolic and mustn't be interpreted literally. Others feel it is a combination of comments equally applied to the destruction of Jerusalem and the return of Christ. Still others state that the chapter has one purpose, and that is to prepare us for the final judgment.

We know two things for sure. First, Jesus is preparing his disciples for a cataclysmic future. His words of disaster rang true in AD 70 when Jerusalem was brought to her knees by the Romans. His words will ring true again when he comes to reclaim his own and put a period after history.

We also know, however, that cataclysms don't occur just in Jerusalem and at the end of history. Hungry bodies and cold hearts are easily found today. The counsel Jesus gives on surviving tough times is useful for more than the battles of Rome and Armageddon. It is useful for the battles of your world and mine.

So if you are looking for my prediction of the day Christ will return, sorry. You won't find it here. He hasn't chosen to give us that date, so time spent speculating is time poorly used.

He has chosen, however, to give a manual of survival for lives under siege.

"As Jesus left the Temple and was walking away, his followers came up to show him the Temple's buildings. Jesus asked, 'Do you see all these buildings? I tell you the truth, not one stone will be left on another. Every stone will be thrown down to the ground'" (Matt. 24:1–2 NCV).

It's impossible to overstate the role of the temple in the Jewish mind. The temple was the meeting place between God and man. It represented the atonement, the sacrifice, and the priesthood. It was the structure that represented the heart of the people.

The temple was dazzling, built with white marble and plated

with gold. In the sun it shone so bright as to test the eyes. The temple area was surrounded by porches, and on these porches were pillars cut out of solid marble in one piece. They were thirty-seven and a half feet high and so thick that three men joining hands could barely encircle one. Archaeologists have found cornerstones from the temple that measure twenty to forty feet in length and weigh more than four hundred tons.[1]

What an impressive sight this must have been for the rural followers of Jesus! Little wonder they were slack-jawed. But more stirring than what they saw was what they heard Jesus say: "I tell you the truth, not one stone will be left on another. Every stone will be thrown down to the ground" (Matt. 24:2 NCV).

There is pathos in the simple phrase that begins the chapter—"Jesus left the Temple and was walking away" (Matt. 24:1 NCV). Jesus has turned his back on the temple.[2] The one who called for the construction of the temple is walking away from it. The Holy One has abandoned the cherished mountain.

He told them, "The whole thing will come crashing down."[3]

To say the temple would crash was to say the nation would crash. The temple was the people. For more than a millennium the temple had been the heart of Israel, and now Jesus was saying the heart would break. "Your house will be left completely empty,"[4] he told the Pharisees earlier in the day.

And crash it did. In AD 70, Titus, the Roman general, laid siege to the city. Being set on a hill, Jerusalem was difficult to take. So Titus resolved to starve it. The grim horror of the famine is a black day in Jewish history. Let the historian Josephus describe the siege:

Then did the famine widen in its progress, and devoured people by whole houses and families; the upper rooms were full of women and children that were dying of famine; and the lanes of the city were full of dead bodies of the aged; the children also and young men wandered about the marketplaces like shadows, all swelled with famine and fell down dead wheresoever their misery seized them. . . . The famine confounded all natural passions; for those who were just going to die looked upon those who were gone to their rest before them with dry eyes and open mouths. A deep silence, also, and a kind of deadly night had seized upon the city . . . and every one of them died with their eyes fixed upon the Temple.[5]

A holocaust: 97,000 were taken captive and 1,100,000 were slain. It was this disaster that Jesus foresaw. It was for this disaster that he prepared his disciples. And it is this type of disaster that can strike your world.

Jesus didn't say, "In this world you may have trouble" or "In this world there are some who have trouble." No, he assured us, "In this world you will have trouble."[6] If you have a pulse, you will have pain. If you are a person, you will have problems.

In Matthew 24 Jesus prepares his disciples by telling them what will happen.

Many will come in my name, saying, "I am the Christ," and they will fool many people. You will hear about wars and stories of wars that are coming, but don't be afraid. These things must happen before the end comes. . . . There will be times when there is no food for people to eat, and there will be earthquakes in different places. These things are like the first pains when something new is about to be born.

Then people will arrest you, hand you over to be hurt, and kill you. They will hate you because you believe in me. (vv. 5–9 NCV)

Jesus is honest about the life we are called to lead. There is no guarantee that just because we belong to him we will go unscathed. No promise is found in Scripture that says when you follow the king you are exempt from battle. No, often just the opposite is the case.

How do we survive the battle? How do we endure the fray?

Jesus gives three certainties. Three assurances. Three absolutes. Imagine him leaning closer and looking deeply into the wide eyes of the disciples. Knowing the jungle they are about to enter, he gives them three compasses that, if used, will keep them on the right trail.

First, assurance of victory: "Those people who keep their faith until the end will be saved" (Matt. 24:13 NCV). He doesn't say if you succeed, you will be saved. Or if you come out on top, you will be saved. He says if you endure. An accurate rendering would be "If you hang in there until the end . . . if you go the distance."

The Brazilians have a great word for this. In Portuguese a person who has the ability to hang in and not give up has *garra*. *Garra* means "claws." What imagery! A person with *garra* has claws that burrow into the side of the cliff and keep him from falling.

So do the saved. They may get close to the edge; they may even stumble and slide. But they will dig their nails into the rock of God and hang on.

Jesus gives you this assurance: If you hang on, he'll make sure you get home.

Second, Jesus gives the assurance of accomplishment: "The Good News about God's kingdom will be preached in all the world, to every nation" (Matt. 24:14 NCV).

Last, Jesus gives us assurance of completion: "Then the end will come" (Matt. 24:14 NCV).

First Thessalonians 4:16 is an intriguing verse: "The Lord himself will come down from heaven, with a loud command."

Have you ever wondered what that command will be? It will be the inaugural word of heaven. It will be the first audible message most have heard from God. It will be the word that closes one age and opens a new one.

I think I know what the command will be. I could very well be wrong, but I think the command that puts an end to the pains of the earth and initiates the joys of heaven will be two words:

"No more."

The King of kings will raise his pierced hand and proclaim, "No more."

The angels will stand, and the Father will speak: "No more."

Every person who lives and who ever lived will turn toward the sky and hear God announce, "No more."

No more loneliness.

No more tears.

No more death. No more sadness. No more crying. No more pain.

As John sat on the island of Patmos, surrounded by sea and separated from friends, he dreamed of the day when God would say, "No more."

This same disciple who, more than half a century before, had heard Jesus speak these words of assurance now knew what they meant. I wonder if he could hear the voice of Jesus in his memory.

"The end will come."

For those who live for this world, that's bad news. But for those who live for the world to come, it's an encouraging promise.

You're in a minefield, my friend, and it's only a matter of time: "In this world you will have trouble. . . ." Next time you ride the rapids of life, remember his words of assurance.

Those who endure will be saved.

The gospel will be preached.

The end will come.

You can count on it.

QUESTIONS FOR REFLECTION

1. As you were growing up, what did your parents, teachers, or pastors teach you about death?
   - How do you view death now?
   - What do you think happens to our spirits when we die?
   - What do think happens to our bodies?
   - How certain are you of this?

2. While the exact location of Jesus' tomb is unknown, some believe it may be located in what is today called the Garden Tomb, a small garden just outside the old city walls of Jerusalem and near a large, skull-shaped rock, believed by some to be Golgotha. The tomb has a small entrance carved

into the side of a rock that leads into a low-ceilinged cave. On one of the walls of the cave is a painted cross from the Crusader era, indicating Christians have been observing this site as the site of Jesus' tomb for hundreds of years.

- Read Matthew 28:2–6.
  - What happened to Jesus' body after the crucifixion?
- Read Philippians 3:20–21.
  - What will happen to our bodies after we die?
  - How do you feel about your body? Do you appreciate your body because it's strong and healthy? Do you dislike your body because it has been sick for a long time? Or do you wish your body was different in some way? If so, how?
  - What would have to change for your body to be "completely whole"?
  - What promise for the future does this Philippians passage offer?
  - How could it change the way you feel about your body today?

3. Read Matthew 24.
   - What imagery stands out to you in this passage?
   - Scholars and theologians have various interpretations for this chapter. What does Max say are the two things we can know for sure about it?

4. The temple was the center of the city of Jerusalem until it fell in AD 70.

- What was the significance of the temple for the Jews?
- What is your "temple"—a cornerstone in your life that should it break, so would you?
- Perhaps your temple has already come down—a life-shattering event that changed everything. What was that experience like for you?

5. What three promises did Jesus give in Matthew 24:13–14? How can these promises give you hope either for a temple-shattering event you've already experienced or a battle you're facing today?

CHAPTER 10

GARDEN MOMENTS

What's your worst fear? A fear of public failure, unemployment, or heights? The fear that you'll never find the right spouse or enjoy good health? The fear of being trapped, abandoned, or forgotten?

These are real fears, born out of legitimate concerns. Yet left unchecked, they metastasize into obsessions. The step between prudence and paranoia is short and steep. Prudence wears a seat belt. Paranoia avoids cars. Prudence washes with soap. Paranoia avoids human contact. Prudence saves for old age. Paranoia hoards even trash. Prudence prepares and plans. Paranoia panics. Prudence calculates the risk and takes the plunge. Paranoia never enters the water.

How many people spend life on the edge of the pool, consulting caution, ignoring faith, and never taking the plunge? Happy to experience life vicariously through others. Preferring to take no risk. For fear of the worst, they never enjoy life at its best.

Jesus was not immune to fear, and he did more than speak about fear. He faced it.

The decisive acts of the gospel drama are played out on two stages—Gethsemane's garden and Golgotha's cross. Friday's cross witnessed the severest suffering. Thursday's garden staged the profoundest fear. It was here, amid the olive trees, that Jesus "fell to the ground. He prayed that, if it were possible, the awful hour awaiting him might pass him by. 'Abba, Father,' he cried out, 'everything is possible for you. Please take this cup of suffering away from me. Yet I want your will to be done, not mine'" (Mark 14:35–36 NLT).

A reader once called me both on the phone and on the carpet because of what I wrote on this passage. He didn't appreciate the way I described Christ as having "eyes wide with a stupor of fear."[1] I told him he needed to take his complaint to a higher level. Gospel-writer Mark is the one who paints the picture of Jesus as pale faced and trembling. "Horror . . . came over him" (Mark 14:33 NEB). The word *horror* is "used of a man who is rendered helpless, disoriented, who is agitated and anguished by the threat of some approaching event."[2]

Matthew agreed. He described Jesus as

depressed and confused (Matt. 26:37[3]);
sorrowful and troubled (RSV);
anguish[ed] and dismay[ed] (NEB).

We've never seen Christ like this. Not in the Galilean storm, at the demoniac's necropolis, or on the edge of the Nazarene cliff.

We've never heard such screams from his voice or seen his eyes this wide. And never, ever, have we read a sentence like this: "He sank into a pit of suffocating darkness" (Mark 14:33 THE MESSAGE). This is a weighty moment. God has become flesh, and Flesh is feeling fear full bore. Why? Of what was Jesus afraid?

It had something to do with a cup. "Take away this cup of suffering" (Luke 22:42 NCV). *Cup*, in biblical terminology, was more than a drinking utensil. *Cup* equaled God's anger, judgment, and punishment. When God took pity on apostate Jerusalem, he said, "See, I have taken out of your hand the cup that made you stagger . . . the goblet of my wrath" (Isa. 51:22). Through Jeremiah, God declared that all nations would drink of the cup of his disgust: "Take from my hand this cup filled to the brim with my anger, and make all the nations to whom I send you drink from it" (Jer. 25:15 NLT). According to John, those who dismiss God "must drink the wine of God's anger. It has been poured full strength into God's cup of wrath. And they will be tormented with fire and burning sulfur in the presence of the holy angels and the Lamb" (Rev. 14:10 NLT).

The cup equaled Jesus' worst-case scenario: to be the recipient of God's wrath. He had never felt God's fury, didn't deserve to. He'd never experienced isolation from his Father; the two had been one for eternity. He'd never known physical death; he was an immortal being. Yet within a few short hours, Jesus would face them all. God would unleash his sin-hating wrath on the sin-covered Son. And Jesus was afraid. Deathly afraid. And what he did with his fear shows us what to do with ours.

He prayed. He told his followers, "Sit here while I go and

pray over there" (Matt. 26:36 NKJV). One prayer was inadequate. "Again, a second time, He went away and prayed . . . and prayed the third time, saying the same words" (vv. 42, 44 NKJV). He even requested the prayer support of his friends. "Stay awake and pray for strength," he urged (v. 41 NCV).

Jesus faced his ultimate fear with honest prayer.

Let's not overcomplicate this topic. Don't we do so? We prescribe words for prayer, places for prayer, clothing for prayer, postures for prayer; durations, intonations, and incantations. Yet Jesus' garden appeal had none of these. It was brief (fewer than twenty-six English words), straightforward ("Please take this cup of suffering away"), and trusting ("Yet I want your will to be done, not mine"). Low on slick and high on authentic. Less a silver-tongued saint in the sanctuary; more a frightened child on a father's lap.

That's it. Jesus' garden prayer is a child's prayer. "Abba," he prayed, using the homespun word a child would use while scampering onto the lap of Papa.

My father let me climb onto his lap . . . when he drove! He'd be arrested for doing so today. I loved it. Did it matter that I couldn't see over the dash? That my feet stopped two feet shy of the brake and accelerator? That I didn't know a radio from a carburetor? By no means. I helped my dad drive his truck.

There were occasions when he even let me select the itinerary. At an intersection he would offer, "Right or left, Max?" I'd lift my freckled face and peer over the steering wheel, consider my options, and make my choice.

And do so with gusto, whipping the wheel like a race car driver at Monte Carlo. Did I fear driving into the ditch? Overturning the curve? Running the tire into a rut? By no means. Dad's hands were next to mine, his eyes keener than mine. Consequently, I was fearless! Anyone can drive a car from the lap of a father.

And anyone can pray from the same perspective.

Prayer is the practice of sitting calmly in God's lap and placing our hands on his steering wheel. He handles the speed and hard curves and ensures safe arrival. And we offer our requests; we ask God to "take this cup away." This cup of disease, betrayal, financial collapse, joblessness, conflict, or senility. Prayer is this simple. And such a simple prayer equipped Christ to stare down his deepest fear.

Do likewise. Fight your dragons in Gethsemane's garden. Those persistent, ugly villains of the heart—talk to God about them.

I don't want to lose my spouse, Lord. Help me to fear less and to trust you more.

I have to fly tomorrow, Lord, and I can't sleep for fear some terrorist will get on board and take down the plane. Won't you remove this fear?

The bank just called and is about to foreclose on our home. What's going to happen to my family? Can you teach me to trust?

I'm scared, Lord. The doctor just called, and the news is not good. You know what's ahead for me. I give my fear to you.

Be specific about your fears. Identify what "this cup" is and talk to God about it. Putting your worries into words disrobes them. They look silly standing there naked.

I must say a word about fear. It is life's only true opponent. Only fear can defeat life. It is a clever, treacherous adversary. How well I know. It has no decency, respects no law or convention, shows no mercy. It goes for your weakest spot, which it finds with unerring ease. It begins in your mind, always. One moment you are feeling calm, self-possessed, happy. Then fear, disguised in the garb of mild-mannered doubt, slips into your mind like a spy. Doubt meets disbelief, and disbelief tries to push it out. But disbelief is a poorly armed foot soldier. Doubt does away with it with little trouble. You become anxious. Reason comes to do battle for you. You are reassured. Reason is fully equipped with the latest weapons technology. But to your amazement, despite superior tactics and a number of undeniable victories, reason is laid low. You feel yourself weakening, wavering. Your anxiety becomes dread. . . .

"Quickly you make rash decisions. You dismiss your last allies: hope and trust. There, you've defeated yourself. Fear, which is but an impression, has triumphed over you."[4]

Fear cannot be reasoned with. Logic doesn't talk fear off the ledge or onto the airplane. So what does? How can one avoid that towel-in-the-ring surrender to the enemy?

It's our duty to pull back the curtains, to expose our fears, each and every one. Like vampires, they can't stand the sunlight. Financial fears, relationship fears, professional fears, safety fears—call them out in prayer. Drag them out by the hand of your mind, and make them stand before God and take their comeuppance!

Jesus made his fears public. He "offered up prayers and petitions with fervent cries and tears to the one who could save him from death" (Heb. 5:7). He prayed loudly enough to be heard and recorded, and he begged his community of friends to pray with him.

His prayer in the garden becomes, for Christians, a picture of the church in action—a place where fears can be verbalized, pronounced, stripped down, and denounced; an escape from the "wordless darkness"[5] of suppressed frights. A healthy church is where our fears go to die. We pierce them through with Scripture, psalms of celebration and lament. We melt them in the sunlight of confession. We extinguish them with the waterfall of worship, choosing to gaze at God, not our dreads.

The next time you find yourself facing a worst-case moment, do this. Verbalize your angst to a trusted circle of God-seekers. This is an essential step. Find your version of Peter, James, and John. The big deal (and good news) is this: you needn't live alone with your fear.

Besides, what if your fears are nothing more than the devil's hoax? A hell-hatched, joy-stealing prank?

As followers of God, you and I have a huge asset. We know everything is going to turn out all right. Christ hasn't budged from his throne, and Romans 8:28 hasn't evaporated from the Bible. Our problems have always been his possibilities. The kidnapping of Joseph resulted in the preservation of his family. The persecution of Daniel led to a cabinet position. Christ entered the world by a surprise pregnancy and redeemed it through his unjust murder. Dare we believe what the Bible teaches? That no disaster is ultimately fatal?

Chrysostom did. He was the archbishop of Constantinople from AD 398 to 404. He gained a following by his eloquent criticisms of the wealthy and powerful. Twice banished by the authorities, he once asked:

> What can I fear? Will it be death? But you know that Christ is my life, and that I shall gain by death. Will it be exile? But the earth and all its fulness is the Lord's. Will it be the loss of wealth? But we have brought nothing into the world, and can carry nothing out. Thus all the terrors of the world are contemptible in my eyes; and I smile at all its good things. Poverty I do not fear; riches I do not sigh for. Death I do not shrink from.[6]

The apostle Paul would have applauded that paragraph. He penned his final words in the bowels of a Roman prison, chained to a guard—within earshot of his executioner's footsteps. Worst-case scenario? Not from Paul's perspective. "God's looking after me, keeping me safe in the kingdom of heaven. All praise to him, praise forever!" (2 Tim. 4:18 THE MESSAGE).

Paul chose to trust his Father.

Aristotle called death the thing to be feared most because "it appears to be the end of everything."[7] Jean-Paul Sartre asserted that death "removes all meaning from life."[8] Robert Green Ingersoll, one of America's most outspoken agnostics, could offer no words of hope at his brother's funeral. He said, "Life is a narrow vale between the cold and barren peaks of two eternities. We strive in vain to look beyond the heights."[9] The pessimism of French philosopher François Rabelais was equally arctic. He made this sentence his final one: "I am going to the great Perhaps."[10] Shakespeare described the afterlife with the gloomiest of terms in Hamlet's line: "The dread of something after death, the undiscover'd country from whose bourn no traveller returns."[11]

Such sad, depressing language! If death is nothing more than "the end of everything," "barren peaks," and "the great Perhaps," what is the possibility of dying bravely? But what if the philosophers missed it? Suppose death is different from the way they thought of it, less a curse and more a passageway, not a crisis to be avoided but a corner to be turned? What if the cemetery is not the dominion of the Grim Reaper but the domain of the Soul Keeper, who will someday announce, "O dwellers in the dust, awake and sing for joy!" (Isa. 26:19 RSV)?

This is the promise of Christ: "Don't let your hearts be troubled. Trust in God, and trust also in me. There is more than enough room in my Father's home. If this were not so, would I have told you that I am going to prepare a place for you? When everything is ready, I will come and get you, so that you will always be with me where I am" (John 14:1–3 NLT).

While Jesus' words sound comforting to us, they sounded radical to his first-century audience. He was promising to accomplish a feat no one dared envision or imagine. He would return from the dead and rescue his followers from the grave.

Traditional Judaism was divided on the topic of resurrection. "For Sadducees say that there is no resurrection—and no angel or spirit; but the Pharisees confess both" (Acts 23:8 NKJV). The Sadducees saw the grave as a tragic, one-way trip into Sheol. No escape. No hope. No possibility of parole. "The living know that they will die, but the dead know nothing" (Eccl. 9:5).

The Pharisees envisioned a resurrection, but the resurrection was spiritual, not physical. "There are no traditions about prophets being raised to a new bodily life. . . . However exalted Abraham, Isaac, and Jacob may have been in Jewish thought, nobody imagined they had been raised from the dead."[12]

Ancient Greek philosophy used different language but resulted in identical despair. Their map of death included the River Styx and the boatman Charon. Upon death the soul of the individual would be ferried across the river and released into a sunless afterlife of bodiless spirits, shades, and shadows.

This was the landscape into which Jesus entered. Yet he walked into this swamp of uncertainty and built a sturdy bridge. He promised not just an afterlife but a better life.

"There are many rooms in my Father's house; . . . I am going there to prepare a place for you" (John 14:2 NCV). We Westerners might miss the wedding images, but you can bet your sweet chuppah that Jesus' listeners didn't. This was a groom-to-bride promise. Upon receiving the permission of both families, the groom returned to the home of his father and built a home for his bride. He "prepared a place."

By promising to do the same for us, Jesus elevates funerals to the same hope level as weddings. From his perspective the trip to the cemetery and the walk down the aisle warrant identical excitement.

Weddings are great news!

So, says Jesus, are burials. Both celebrate a new era, name, and home. In both the groom walks the bride away on his arm. Jesus is your coming groom. "I will come and get you . . ." He will meet you at the altar. Your final glimpse of life will trigger your first glimpse of him.

QUESTIONS FOR REFLECTION

1. What is your worst fear?
   - Why is this your worst fear?
   - When did this fear begin?

2. Read Mark 14:32–35. How was Jesus feeling in the garden of Gethsemane, the garden that overlooked the city of Jerusalem?
   - When is the last time you felt the way Jesus did—deeply troubled, distressed, or crushed by grief?
   - How does it make you feel to know that Jesus felt the same way?

3. What does a cup symbolize in biblical terminology?
   - What did it represent for Jesus specifically?
   - What did Jesus do with the cup he had been given?
   - Fill in the blank: "Jesus' garden prayer is a ___ prayer" (p. 147).
   - What "cup" do you want taken from you today?
   - Is this cup related to your worst fear from question 1?
   - How could you pray for your cup in the same way Jesus did in the garden?

4. Read John 14:1–3. How would Jesus' first-century audience understand this differently than we do?
   - What do you think about the imagery of Jesus as our bridegroom, preparing a home for us?
   - How could this passage give you hope in the face of your greatest fear?

CHAPTER 11

GRIEVING AND HOPING

Y ou are leaving the church building. The funeral is over. The
burial is next. Ahead of you walk six men who carry the coffin
that carries the body of your son. Your only son.

You're numb from the sorrow. Stunned. You lost your husband,
and now you've lost your son. Now you have no family. If you had
any more tears, you'd weep. If you had any more faith, you'd pray.
But both are in short supply, so you do neither. You just stare at the
back of the wooden box.

Suddenly it stops. The pallbearers have stopped. You stop.

A man has stepped in front of the casket. You don't know him.
You've never seen him. He wasn't at the funeral. He's dressed in a

corduroy coat and jeans. You have no idea what he is doing. But before you can object, he steps up to you and says, "Don't cry."

Don't cry? Don't cry! This is a funeral. My son is dead. Don't cry? Who are you to tell me not to cry? Those are your thoughts, but they never become your words. Because before you can speak, he acts.

He turns back to the coffin, places his hand on it, and says in a loud voice, "Young man, I tell you, get up!"

"Now just a minute," one of the pallbearers objects. But the sentence is interrupted by a sudden movement in the casket. The men look at one another and lower it quickly to the ground. It's a good thing they do, because as soon as it touches the sidewalk, the lid slowly opens . . .

Sound like something out of a science fiction novel? It's not. It's right out of the gospel of Luke. "He went up and touched the coffin, and the people who were carrying it stopped. Jesus said, 'Young man, I tell you, get up!' And the son sat up and began to talk" (Luke 7:14–15 NCV).

Now the question. What's odd about that verse?

You got it. Dead people don't sit up! Dead people don't talk! Dead people don't leave their coffins!

Unless Jesus shows up. Because when Jesus shows up, you never know what might happen.

Jairus can tell you. His daughter was already dead. The mourners were already in the house. The funeral had begun. The people thought the best Jesus could do was offer some kind words about Jairus's girl. Jesus had some words all right. Not about the girl, but for the girl.

"My child, stand up!" (Luke 8:54 NCV).

The next thing the father knew, she was eating, Jesus was laughing, and the hired mourners were sent home early.

Martha can tell you. She'd hoped Jesus would show up to heal Lazarus. He didn't. Then she'd hoped he'd show up to bury Lazarus. He didn't. By the time he made it to Bethany, Lazarus was four-days buried, and Martha was wondering what kind of friend Jesus was.

She hears he's at the edge of town, so she storms out to meet him. "Lord, if you had been here," she confronts, "my brother would not have died" (John 11:21 NCV).

There is hurt in those words. Hurt and disappointment. The one man who could have made a difference didn't, and Martha wants to know why.

Maybe you do too. Maybe you've done what Martha did. Someone you love ventures near the edge of life, and you turn to Jesus for help. You, like Martha, turn to the only one who can pull a person from the ledge of death. You ask Jesus to give a hand.

But when Martha asked, he didn't come. Lazarus got worse. She watched out the window. Jesus didn't show. Her brother drifted in and out of consciousness. "He'll be here soon, Lazarus," she promised. "Hang on."

But the knock at the door never came. Jesus never appeared. Not to help. Not to heal. Not to bury. And now, four days later, he finally shows up. The funeral is over. The body is buried, and the grave is sealed.

And Martha is hurt.

Her words have been echoed in a thousand cemeteries. "If you had been here, my brother would not have died."

If you were doing your part, God, my husband would have survived. If you'd done what was right, Lord, my baby would have lived.

If only you had heard my prayer, God, my arms wouldn't be empty.

The grave unearths our view of God.

When we face death, our definition of God is challenged. Which, in turn, challenges our faith. Which leads me to ask a grave question. Why is it that we interpret the presence of death as the absence of God? Why do we think that if the body is not healed, then God is not near? Is healing the only way God demonstrates his presence?

Sometimes we think so. And as a result, when God doesn't answer our prayers for healing, we get angry. Resentful. Blame replaces belief. "If you had been here, doing your part, God, then this death would not have happened."

It's distressing that this view of God has no place for death.

Please understand, Jesus didn't raise the dead for the sake of the dead. He raised the dead for the sake of the living.

"Lazarus, come out!" (11:43 NCV).

Martha was silent as Jesus commanded. The mourners were quiet. No one stirred as Jesus stood face-to-face with the rock-hewn tomb and demanded that it release his friend.

No one stirred, that is except for Lazarus. Deep within the tomb he moved. His stilled heart began to beat again. Wrapped eyes popped open. Wooden fingers lifted. And a mummied man in a tomb sat up. Want to know what happened next?

Let John tell you. "The dead man came out, his hands and feet wrapped with pieces of cloth, and a cloth around his face" (v. 44).

There it is again. Five words.

"The dead man came out."

Can I ask the same questions?

Question: What's wrong with this picture?

Answer: Dead men don't walk out of tombs.

Question: What kind of God is this?

Answer: The God who holds the keys to life and death.

The kind of God who rolls back the sleeve of the trickster and reveals death for the parlor trick it is.

The kind of God you want present at your funeral.

He'll do it again, you know. He's promised he would. And he's shown that he can.

"The Lord himself will come down from heaven, with a loud command" (1 Thess. 4:16).

The same voice that awoke the boy near Nain, that stirred the still daughter of Jairus, that awakened the corpse of Lazarus—the same voice will speak again. The earth and the sea will give up their dead. There will be no more death.

Jesus made sure of that.

TRUSTING HIM

The journey from heaven to earth was a long one, but Jesus took it. Why?

He wants us to trust him.

Explore this thought with me for just a moment. Why did Jesus live on the earth as long as he did? Couldn't his life have been much shorter? Why not step into our world just long enough to die for our sins and then leave? Why not a sinless year or week? Why did he have to live a life? To take on our sins is one thing, but to take on our sunburns, our sore throats? To experience death, yes—but to put up with life? To put up with long roads, long days, and short tempers? Why did he do it?

Because he wants you to trust him.

Even his final act on earth was intended to win your trust.

Later, knowing that everything had now been finished, and so that Scripture would be fulfilled, Jesus said, "I am thirsty." A jar of wine vinegar was there, so they soaked a sponge in it, put the sponge on a stalk of the hyssop plant, and lifted it to Jesus' lips. When he had received the drink, Jesus said, "It is finished." With that, he bowed his head and gave up his spirit. (John 19:28–30)

This is the final act of Jesus' life. In the concluding measure of his earthly composition, we hear the sounds of a thirsty man.

And through his thirst—through a sponge and a jar of cheap wine—he leaves a final appeal.

"You can trust me."

Jesus. Lips cracked and mouth of cotton. Throat so dry he couldn't swallow, and voice so hoarse he could scarcely speak. He is thirsty. To find the last time moisture touched these lips you

161

need to rewind a dozen hours to the meal in the upper room. Since tasting that cup of wine, Jesus has been beaten, spat upon, bruised, and cut. He has been a cross-carrier and sin-bearer, and no liquid has salved his throat. He is thirsty.

Why doesn't he do something about it? Couldn't he? Did he not cause jugs of water to become jugs of wine? Did he not make a wall out of the Jordan River and two walls out of the Red Sea? Didn't he, with one word, banish the rain and calm the waves? Doesn't Scripture say that he "turned the desert into pools" (Ps. 107:35) and "the hard rock into springs" (Ps. 114:8)?

Did God not say, "I will pour water on him who is thirsty" (Isa. 44:3 NKJV)?

If so, why does Jesus endure thirst?

While we are asking this question, add a few more. Why did he grow weary in Samaria (John 4:6), disturbed in Nazareth (Mark 6:6), and angry in the Temple (John 2:15)? Why was he sleepy in the boat on the Sea of Galilee (Mark 4:38), sad at the tomb of Lazarus (John 11:35), and hungry in the wilderness (Matt. 4:2)?

Why? And why did he grow thirsty on the cross?

He didn't have to suffer thirst. At least not to the level he did. Six hours earlier he'd been offered drink, but he refused it.

They brought Jesus to the place called Golgotha (which means "the place of the skull"). Then they offered him wine mixed with myrrh, but he did not take it. And they crucified him. Dividing up his clothes, they cast lots to see what each would get. (Mark 15:22–24)

Before the nail was pounded, a drink was offered. Mark says the wine was mixed with myrrh. Matthew described it as wine mixed with gall. Both myrrh and gall contain sedative properties that numb the senses. But Jesus refused them. He refused to be stupefied by the drugs, opting instead to feel the full force of his suffering.

Why? Why did he endure all these feelings? *Because he knew you would feel them too.*

He knew you would be weary, disturbed, and angry. He knew you'd be sleepy, grief-stricken, and hungry. He knew you'd face pain. If not the pain of the body, the pain of the soul . . . pain too sharp for any drug. He knew you'd face thirst. If not a thirst for water, at least a thirst for truth, and the truth we glean from the image of a thirsty Christ is—he understands.

And because he understands, we can come to him.

Wouldn't his lack of understanding keep us from him? Doesn't the lack of understanding keep us from others? Suppose you were discouraged at your financial state. You need some guidance from a sympathetic friend. Would you go to the son of a zillionaire? Would you approach someone who inherited a fortune? Probably not. Why? He would not understand. He's likely never been where you are, so he can't relate to how you feel.

Jesus, however, has and can. He has been where you are and can relate to how you feel. And if his life on earth doesn't convince you, his death on the cross should. He understands what you are going through. Our Lord does not patronize us or scoff at our needs. He responds "generously to all without finding fault" (James 1:5). How can he do this? No one penned it more clearly than did the author of Hebrews.

Jesus understands every weakness of ours, because he was tempted in every way that we are. But he did not sin! So whenever we are in need, we should come bravely before the throne of our merciful God. There we will be treated with undeserved grace, and we will find help. (Heb. 4:15–16 CEV)

Why did the throat of heaven grow raw? So we would know that he understands, so all who struggle would hear his invitation: "You can trust me."

The word *trust* does not appear in the passage about the wine and sponge, but we do find a phrase that makes it easier to trust. Look at the sentence prior to the declaration of thirst: "So that Scripture would be fulfilled, Jesus said, 'I am thirsty'" (John 19:28). In that verse John gives us the motive behind Jesus' words. Our Lord was concerned with the fulfillment of Scripture. In fact, the fulfillment of Scripture is a recurring theme in the passion.

Consider this list:

The betrayal of Jesus by Judas occurred "to bring about what the Scripture said." (John 13:18 NCV; John 17:12)

The gamble for the clothing took place "so that this Scripture would come true: 'They divided my clothes among them, and they threw lots for my clothing.'" (John 19:24 NCV)

The legs of Christ were not broken "to make the Scripture come true: 'Not one of his bones will be broken.'" (John 19:36 NCV)

The side of Jesus was pierced to fulfill the passage that says, "They will look at the one they stabbed." (John 19:37 NCV)

John says the disciples were stunned by the empty tomb since "they did not yet understand from the Scriptures that Jesus must rise from the dead." (John 20:9 NCV)

Why the recurring references to Scripture? Why, in his final moments, was Jesus determined to fulfill prophecy? He knew we would doubt. He knew we would question. And since he did not want our heads to keep his love from our hearts, he used his final moments to offer proof that he was the Messiah. He systematically fulfilled centuries-old prophecies.

Every important detail of the great tragedy had been written down beforehand:

- the betrayal by a familiar friend (Ps. 41:9)
- the forsaking of the disciples through being offended at him (Ps. 31:11)
- the false accusation (Ps. 35:11)
- the silence before his judges (Isa. 53:7)
- being proven guiltless (Isa. 53:9)
- being included with sinners (Isa. 53:12)
- being crucified (Ps. 22:16)
- the mockery of the spectators (Ps. 109:25)
- the taunt of non-deliverance (Ps. 22:7–8)
- the gambling for his garments (Ps. 22:18)

- the prayer for his enemies (Isa. 53:12)
- being forsaken by God (Ps. 22:1)
- the yielding of his spirit into the hands of his Father (Ps. 31:5)
- the bones not broken (Ps. 34:20)
- the burial in a rich man's tomb (Isa. 53:9)

Did you know that in his life Christ fulfilled 351 distinct prophecies in the Old Testament?[1] What are the mathematical possibilities of all these prophecies being fulfilled in the life of one man?

Why did Jesus proclaim his thirst from the cross? To lay just one more plank on a sturdy bridge over which a doubter could walk. His confession of thirst is a signal for all who seek it—he is the Messiah.

His final act, then, is a warm word for the cautious: "You can trust in me."

Don't we need someone to trust? And don't we need someone to trust who is bigger than we are? Aren't we tired of trusting the people of this earth for understanding? Aren't we weary of trusting the things of this earth for strength?

Jesus' message through the wine-soaked sponge is this: I am that person. Trust me.

QUESTIONS FOR REFLECTION

1. Jesus performed three resurrection miracles in Scripture (not including his own resurrection). You've already learned about

Lazarus at Bethany and Jairus's daughter in Capernaum. Read about the widow's son Jesus raised to life near the city of Nain, a town southeast of Nazareth and only mentioned once in the Bible. Read Luke 7:11–17.

- The woman was a widow, so she had already lost her husband. What would be the consequences if her son also died?

- Have you experienced multiples losses in a row, whether that was losing people you loved or another type of loss? What was that experience like for you?

- Unlike Jairus, who pleaded with Jesus to heal his daughter, and unlike Mary and Martha, who already had a relationship with Jesus, Jesus seemed to not know the widow in this story, and she didn't ask Jesus for help. Why do you think Jesus decided to raise her son from the dead?

- What does this story tell you about how Jesus feels about the losses we experience in life and what he can do with our loss?

2. How would you gauge your level of trust in Jesus today? Do you trust him all the time? Sometimes? For certain things but not for others? Explain your answer.

- Why is it important to have people in our lives we can trust?

- When has your trust in someone been broken?

- What was that experience like?

- How did it affect your relationship with him or her?

- Has your trust in Jesus ever been broken? If so, when, and how has this affected your relationship with him?

3. While Jesus hung on the cross at Golgotha, he was offered wine mixed with myrrh.
   - Why was he offered this?
   - Why did he refuse it?
   - Does knowing that Jesus experienced life on earth and the physical and emotional pain that comes with it affect your trust in him? If so, how?

4. How many prophecies did Jesus fulfill and why does this matter?

5. What do you need in order to trust Jesus more?

CHAPTER 12

DEATH DEFEATED

The hill is quiet now. Not still but quiet. For the first time all day there is no noise. The clamor began to subside when the darkness—that puzzling midday darkness—fell. Like water douses a fire, the shadows doused the ridicule. No more taunts. No more jokes. No more jesting. And, in time, no more mockers. One by one the onlookers turned and began the descent.

That is, all the onlookers except you and me. We did not leave. We came to learn. And so we lingered in the semidarkness and listened. We listened to the soldiers cursing, the passersby questioning, and the women weeping. But most of all we listened to the trio of dying men groaning. Hoarse, guttural, thirsty groans. They groaned with each roll of the head and each pivot of the legs.

But as the minutes became hours, these groans diminished.

The three seemed dead. Were it not for the belabored breathing, you would have thought they were.

Then he screamed. As if someone had yanked his hair, the back of his head slammed against the sign that bore his name, and he screamed. Like a dagger cuts the curtain, his scream cut the dark. Standing as straight as the nails would permit, he cried as one calling for a lost friend, *"Eloi!"*

His voice was raspy, scratchy. Reflections of the torch flame danced in his wide eyes. "My God!"

Ignoring the volcano of erupting pain, he pushed upward until his shoulders were higher than his nailed hands. "Why have you forsaken me?"

The soldiers stared. The weeping of the women ceased. One of the Pharisees sneered sarcastically, "He's calling Elijah."

No one laughed.

He'd shouted a question to the heavens, and you half expected heaven to shout one in return.

And apparently it did. For the face of Jesus softened, and an afternoon dawn broke as he spoke a final time. "It is finished. Father, into your hands I commit my spirit."[1]

As he gave his final breath, the earth gave a sudden stir. A rock rolled, and a soldier stumbled. Then, as suddenly as the silence was broken, the silence returned.

And now all is quiet. The mocking has ceased. There is no one to mock.

The soldiers are busy with the business of cleaning up the dead. Two men have come. Dressed well and meaning well, they are given the body of Jesus.

And we are left with the relics of his death.

Three nails in a bin.

Three cross-shaped shadows.

A braided crown with scarlet tips.

Bizarre, isn't it? The thought that this blood is not man's blood but God's?

Crazy, isn't it? To think that these nails held your sins to a cross?

Absurd, don't you agree? That a scoundrel's prayer was offered and answered? Or more absurd that another scoundrel offered no prayer at all?

Absurdities and ironies. The hill of Calvary is nothing if not both.

We would have scripted the moment differently. Ask us how a God should redeem his world, and we will show you! White horses, flashing swords. Evil flat on his back. God on his throne.

But God on a cross?

A split-lipped, puffy-eyed, blood-masked God on a cross?

Sponge thrust in his face?

Spear plunged in his side?

Dice tossed at his feet?

No, we wouldn't have written the drama of redemption this way. But, then again, we weren't asked to. These players and props were heaven picked and God ordained. We were not asked to design the hour.

But we have been asked to respond to it. In order for the cross of Christ to be the cross of your life, you and I need to bring something to the hill.

We have seen what Jesus brought. With scarred hands he offered forgiveness. Through torn skin he promised acceptance. He took the path to take us home. He wore our garment to give us his own. We have seen the gifts he brought.

Now we ask, what will we bring?

We aren't asked to paint the sign or carry the nails. We aren't asked to wear the spit or bear the crown. But we are asked to walk the path and leave something at the cross.

We don't have to, of course. Many don't.

Many have done what we have done: More minds than ours have read about the cross; better minds than mine have written about it. Many have pondered what Christ left; fewer have pondered what we must leave.

May I urge you to leave something at the cross? You can observe the cross and analyze the cross. You can read about it, even pray to it. But until you leave something there, you haven't embraced the cross.

You've seen what Christ left. Won't you leave something as well? Why don't you start with your bad moments?

Those bad habits? Leave them at the cross. Your selfish moods and white lies? Give them to God. Your binges and bigotries? God wants them all. Every flop, every failure. He wants every single one. Why? Because he knows we can't live with them.

Listen to his promise:

"This is my commitment to my people: removal of their sins" (Rom. 11:27 THE MESSAGE).

God does more than forgive our mistakes; he removes them! We simply have to take them to him.

He not only wants the mistakes we've made. He wants the ones we are making! Are you making some? Are you drinking too much? Are you cheating at work or cheating at marriage? Are you mismanaging money? Are you mismanaging your life?

If so, don't pretend nothing is wrong. Don't pretend you don't fall. Don't try to get back in the game. Go first to God. The first step after a stumble must be in the direction of the cross. "If we confess our sins to God, he can always be trusted to forgive us and take our sins away" (1 John 1:9 CEV).

What can you leave at the cross? Start with your bad moments. And while you are there, give God your mad moments.

You've already learned, haven't you, that a promise made is not always a promise kept? Just because someone is called your dad, that doesn't mean he will act like your dad. Even though they said "yes" at the altar, they may say "no" in the marriage.

You've already learned, haven't you, that we tend to fight back? To bite back? To keep lists and snarl lips and growl at people we don't like?

God wants your list. He inspired one servant to write, "Love does not keep a record of wrongs" (1 Cor. 13:5 GNT). He wants us to leave the list at the cross.

Not easy.

"Just look what they did to me!" we defy and point to our hurts.

"Just look what I did for you," he reminds and points to the cross.

Paul said it this way: "If someone does wrong to you, forgive that person because the Lord forgave you" (Col. 3:13 NCV).

You and I are commanded—not urged, *commanded*—to keep no list of wrongs.

Besides, do you really want to keep one? Do you really want to catalog all your mistreatments? Do you really want to growl and snap your way through life? God doesn't want you to either. Give up your sins before they infect you and your bitterness before it incites you, and give God your anxiety before it inhibits you. Give God your *anxious moments.*

What do we do with these worries? Take your anxieties to the cross—literally. Next time you're worried about your health or house or finances or flights, take a mental trip up the hill. Spend a few moments looking again at the pieces of the Passion.

Run your thumb over the tip of the spear. Balance a spike in the palm of your hand. Read the wooden sign written in your own language. And as you do, touch the velvet dirt, moist with the blood of God.

Blood he bled for you.

The spear he took for you.

The nails he felt for you.

The sign he left for you.

He did all of this for you. Knowing this, knowing all he did for you there, don't you think he'll look out for you here?

Or as Paul wrote, "God did not keep back his own Son, but he gave him for us. If God did this, won't he freely give us everything else?" (Rom. 8:32 CEV).

Do yourself a favor; take your anxious moments to the cross. Leave them there with your bad moments and your mad moments. And may I suggest one more? Your final moment.

Barring the return of Christ first, you and I will have one. A final moment. A final breath. A final widening of the eyes and beating of the heart. In a split second you'll leave what you know and enter what you don't.

That's what bothers us. Death is the great unknown. We're always a bit skittish about the unknown.

LIFTING THE SHADOW OF DOUBT

Sometimes I can relate to the fear that God isn't. The fear that "why?" has no answer. The fear of a pathless life. The fear that the status quo is as good as it gets. The chilling, quiet, horrifying shadows of aloneness in a valley that emerges from and leads into a fog-covered curve.

The valley of the shadow of doubt.

Perhaps you know its gray terrain? In it

- the Bible reads like *Aesop's Fables*;
- prayers bounce back like cavern echoes;
- moral boundaries are mapped in pencil;
- believers are alternately pitied or envied; someone is deluded.

But who?

To one degree or another we all venture into the valley. At one point or another we all need a plan to escape it. May I share mine? Those Sunday morning sessions of second-guessing dissipate quickly these days thanks to a small masterpiece, a wellspring of faith bubbling in the final pages of Luke's gospel. The physician-turned-historian dedicated his last chapter to answering one question: How does Christ respond when we doubt him?

He takes us to the upper room in Jerusalem. It's Sunday morning following Friday's crucifixion. Jesus' followers have gathered, not to change the world, but to escape it; not as gospel raconteurs, but as scared rabbits. They'd buried their hopes with the carpenter's corpse. You'd have found more courage in a chicken coop and backbone in a jellyfish. Fearless faith? Not here. Search the bearded faces of these men for a glint of resolve, a hint of courage—you'll come up empty.

One look at the bright faces of the females, however, and your heart will leap with theirs. According to Luke they exploded into the room like the sunrise, announcing a Jesus-sighting.

[The women] rushed back from the tomb to tell his eleven disciples—and everyone else—what had happened. It was Mary Magdalene, Joanna, Mary the mother of James, and several other women who told the apostles what had happened. But the story sounded like nonsense to the men, so they didn't believe it. (Luke 24:9–11 NLT)

Periodic doubters of Christ, take note and take heart. The charter followers of Christ had doubts too. But Christ refused to leave them alone with their questions. He, as it turned out, was anything but dead and buried. When he spotted two of the disciples trudging toward a village called Emmaus,

Jesus himself came up and walked along with them; but they were kept from recognizing him. He asked them, "What are you discussing together as you walk along?" They stood still, their faces downcast. (vv. 15–17)

For this assignment angels wouldn't do, an emissary wouldn't suffice, an army of heaven's best soldiers wouldn't be sent. Jesus himself came to the rescue.

And how did he bolster the disciples' faith? A thousand and one tools awaited his bidding. He had marked Friday's crucifixion with an earthquake and a solar eclipse. Matthew's gospel reveals that "saints who had fallen asleep were raised; and coming out of the graves after His resurrection, they went into the holy city and appeared to many" (27:52–53 NKJV). Christ could have summoned a few of them to chat with the Emmaus disciples. Or he could have toured them through the empty tomb. For that matter he could have made the rocks speak or a fig tree dance a jig. But Christ did none of these things. What did he do? "Jesus took them through the writings of Moses and all the prophets, explaining from all the Scriptures the things concerning himself" (Luke 24:27 NLT).

Well, what do you know. Christ conducted a Bible class. He led the Emmaus-bound duo through an Old Testament survey course, from the writings of Moses (Genesis through Deuteronomy) into the messages of Isaiah, Amos, and the others. He turned the Emmaus trail into a biblical time line, pausing to describe . . . the Red Sea rumbling? Jericho tumbling? King David stumbling? Of special import to Jesus were the "Scriptures . . . concerning himself." His face watermarks more Old Testament stories than you might imagine. Jesus is Noah, saving humanity from disaster; Abraham, the father of a new nation; Isaac, placed on the altar by his father; Joseph, sold for a bag of silver; Moses, calling slaves to freedom; Joshua, pointing out the promised land. Jesus "took them through the writings of Moses and all the prophets." Can you imagine Christ quoting Old Testament scripture? Did Isaiah 53 sound this way: "I was wounded and crushed for your sins. I was beaten that you might have peace" (v. 5)? Or Isaiah 28: "I am placing a foundation stone in Jerusalem. It is firm, a tested and precious cornerstone that is safe to build on" (v. 16)? Did he pause and give the Emmaus students a wink, saying, "I'm the stone Isaiah described"? We don't know his words, but we know their impact. The two disciples said they felt "our hearts burning within us while he talked" (Luke 24:32).

By now the trio had crossed northwesterly out of the rocky hills into a scented, gardened valley of olive groves and luscious fruit trees. Jerusalem's grief and bloodshed lay to their backs, forgotten in the conversation. The seven-mile hike felt more like a half-hour stroll. All too quickly fled the moments; the disciples wanted to hear more. "By this time they were nearing Emmaus and the end of their journey. Jesus acted as if he were going on, but they begged him, 'Stay the night with us.' . . . As they sat down to eat, he took the bread and blessed it. Then he broke it and gave it to them. Suddenly, their eyes were opened, and they recognized him. And at that moment he disappeared!" (vv. 28–31 NLT).

Jesus taught the Word and broke the bread, and then like a mist on a July morning, he was gone. The Emmaus pilgrims weren't far behind. The pair dropped the broken loaf, grabbed their broken dreams, raced back to Jerusalem, and burst in on the apostles. They blurted out their discovery, only to be interrupted and upstaged by Jesus himself.

And just as they were telling about it, Jesus himself was suddenly standing there among them. "Peace be with you," he said. But the whole group was startled and frightened, thinking they were seeing a ghost!

"Why are you frightened?" he asked. "Why are your hearts filled with doubt? Look at my hands. Look at my feet. You can see that it's really me. Touch me and make sure that I am not a ghost, because ghosts don't have bodies, as you see that I do." As he spoke, he showed them his hands and his feet.

Still they stood there in disbelief, filled with joy and wonder. Then he asked them, "Do you have anything here to eat?" They gave him a piece of broiled fish, and he ate it as they watched.

Then he said, "When I was with you before, I told you that everything written about me in the law of Moses and the prophets and in the Psalms must be fulfilled." Then he opened their minds to understand the Scriptures. (vv. 36–45 NLT)

The disciples didn't know whether to kneel and worship or to turn tail and run. Someone decided the moment was too good to be true and called Jesus a ghost. Christ could have taken offense. After all, he'd passed through hell itself to save them, and they couldn't differentiate between him and Casper's cousin? But ever patient, as he is with doubters, Jesus extended first one hand, then the other. Then an invitation: "Touch me." He asked for food, and between bites of broiled fish, Jesus initiated his second Bible lesson of the day. "'Everything I told you while I was with you comes to this: All the things written about me in the Law of Moses, in the Prophets, and in the Psalms have to be fulfilled.' He went on to open their understanding of the Word of God, showing them how to read their Bibles this way" (Luke 24:44–45 THE MESSAGE).

We're detecting a pattern, aren't we?

Jesus spots two people lumbering toward Emmaus, both looking as if they had just buried a best friend. Christ either catches up or beams down to them . . . we don't know. He raises the topic of the garden of Eden and the book of Genesis. Next thing you know, a meal is eaten, their hearts are warmed, and their eyes are open.

Jesus pays a visit to the cowardly lions of the upper room. Not a Superman-in-the-sky flyover, mind you. But a face-to-face, put-your-hand-on-my-wound visit. A meal is served, the Bible is taught, the disciples find courage, and we find two practical answers to the critical question, What would Christ have us do with our doubts?

His answer? Touch my body and ponder my story.

We still can, you know. We can still touch the body of Christ. We'd love to touch his physical wounds and feel the flesh of the Nazarene. Yet when we brush up against the church, we do just that. "The church is his body; it is made full and complete by Christ, who fills all things everywhere with himself" (Eph. 1:23 NLT).

Questions can make hermits out of us, driving us into hiding. Yet the cave has no answers. Christ distributes courage through community; he dissipates doubts through fellowship. He never deposits all knowledge in one person but distributes pieces of the jigsaw puzzle to many. When you interlock your understanding with mine, and we share our discoveries . . . When we mix, mingle, confess, and pray, Christ speaks.

The adhesiveness of the disciples instructs us. They stuck together. Even with ransacked hopes, they clustered in conversant community. They kept "going over all these things that had happened" (Luke 24:14 THE MESSAGE). Isn't this a picture of the church—sharing notes, exchanging ideas, mulling over possibilities, lifting spirits? And as they did, Jesus showed up to teach them, proving that "when two or three of you are together because of me, you can be sure that I'll be there" (Matt. 18:20 THE MESSAGE).

And when he speaks, he shares his story. God's go-to therapy for doubters is his own Word. "Before you trust, you have to listen. But unless Christ's Word is preached, there's nothing to listen to" (Rom. 10:17 THE MESSAGE). So listen to it.

Could it be this simple? Could the chasm between doubt and faith be spanned with Scripture and fellowship? Find out for yourself. Next time the shadows come, immerse yourself in the ancient stories of Moses, the prayers of David, the testimonies of the Gospels, and the epistles of Paul. Join with other seekers, and make daily walks to Emmaus. And if a kind stranger joins you on the road with wise teaching . . . consider inviting him over for dinner.

QUESTIONS FOR REFLECTION

1. We know what Jesus brought to the cross on the Hill of Calvary (*Calvary* is the Latin translation for skull): forgiveness for all mankind.
   - What is on your list of sins or grievances you need to bring to the cross?
   - What is on your list of anxieties?
   - What holds you back from bringing these before Christ?

2. After his resurrection, Jesus met two of his disciples while they were walking to Emmaus, a town seven miles west of Jerusalem. Jesus asked them what they were talking about. Read their response in Luke 24:19–24.
   - How did the disciples feel about the death of Jesus?
   - What did they think about his rumored resurrection?
   - When have you experienced doubt in your faith, whether that was in Christ's resurrection or something else?
   - Read Luke 24:27–31. What did Jesus do in response to the disciples' doubt?

3. Jesus appeared to his disciples in Jerusalem soon after he had appeared to the disciples on the road to Emmaus. Read Luke 24:35–45.
   - How did Jesus respond to the disciples' fear and doubt in this passage?

- Why do you think he asked the disciples for food?
- How does this story parallel the story from Emmaus?

4. How can we still touch Jesus' body and ponder his story?
   - Why is community helpful during seasons of doubt?
   - What role has community played in your experiences with doubt in the past?
   - Do you currently have any doubts about your faith? If so, what are they?
   - If so, how could community help support you in those doubts? If not, how could you help someone who has doubts?

NOTES

CHAPTER 1
1. Luke 1:33.

CHAPTER 4
1. Bradford Torrey (ca. 1875), "*Not So in Haste, My Heart,*" Hymnary.org, https://hymnary.org/text/not_so_in_haste_my_heart?extended=true.

CHAPTER 5
1. David M. Howard Jr., *Joshua,* vol. 5, *The New American Commentary* (Nashville: Broadman & Holman, 2002), 212.
2. F. B Meyer, *Joshua, and the Land of Promise* (London: Morgan and Scott, 1870), 96.
3. See also Deuteronomy 27.
4. C. S. Lewis, *Yours, Jack: Spiritual Direction from C. S. Lewis* (New York: HarperCollins, 2008), 152.

CHAPTER 6
1. Matthew 14:22–25.
2. Tracey Gardone, "Eleven Days Versus 40 Years," *Greene County Messenger,*

https://www.heraldstandard.com/gcm/opinion/guest_columnists/eleven
-days-versus-40-years/article_64d00246-60b5-5ce4-a7fd-3159c6d60192
.html.

CHAPTER 7

1. Thomas Lake, "The Way It Should Be: The Story of an Athlete's Singular
   Gesture Continues to Inspire. Careful, Though, It Will Make You Cry,"
   Sports Illustrated, June 29, 2009, www.si.com/vault/2009/06/29
   /105832485/the-way-it-should-be.
2. Ibid.
3. Judas is an example of one who seemed to have been saved but in truth
   was not. For three years he followed Christ. While the others were
   becoming apostles, he was becoming a tool of Satan. When Jesus said,
   "You are clean, though not every one of you" (John 13:10), he was
   referring to Judas, who possessed a fake faith. Persistent sin can betray
   nonbelief.

CHAPTER 9

1. William Barclay, *The Gospel of Matthew*, Vol. 2, *Daily Study Bible Revised
   Edition* (Philadelphia, PA: Westminster Press, 1975), 305.
2. The imperfect tense is used, implying a continual, unending course of
   action.
3. Matthew 24:2. Author's paraphrase.
4. Matthew 23:38 NCV.
5. Barclay, *The Gospel of Matthew*, 307.
6. John 16:33.

CHAPTER 10

1. Max Lucado, *No Wonder They Call Him the Savior* (Nashville, TN:
   Thomas Nelson, 2004), 105.
2. Pierre Benoit, *The Passion and Resurrection of Jesus Christ*, trans. Benet
   Weatherhead (New York: Herder and Herder, 1969), 10, as quoted by
   Frederick Dale Bruner, *Matthew: A Commentary*, vol. 2, *The Churchbook*:
   Matthew 13–28 (Dallas: Word Publishing, 1990), 979.

3. Bruner, *The Churchbook*, 978.

4. Yann Martel, *Life of Pi* (Orlando, FL: Harcourt, 2001), 160. Copyright by Yann Martel. Reprinted by permission of Houghton Mifflin, Harcourt Publishing Company.

5. Ibid.

6. Robert Wheler Bush, *The Life and Times of Chrysostom* (London, England: Religious Tract Society, 1885), 245.

7. Donald G. Bloesch, *The Last Things: Resurrection, Judgment, Glory* (Downers Grove, IL: InterVarsity Press, 2004), 125.

8. Ibid.

9. John Blanchard, *Whatever Happened to Hell?* (Wheaton, IL: Crossway Books, 1995), 63.

10. Ibid, 62.

11. William Shakespeare, *Hamlet*, in *The Complete Works of Shakespeare,* ed. Hardin Craig (Glenview, IL: Scott, Foresman and Company, 1961), 3.1.78–80. References are to act, scene, and line.

12. N. T. Wright, *Christian Origins and the Question of God*, vol. 3, *The Resurrection of the Son of God* (Minneapolis: Fortress Press, 2003), 205–6.

CHAPTER 11

1. "351 Old Testament Prophecies Fulfilled in Jesus Christ," https://www.newtestamentchristians.com/bible-study-resources/351-old-testament-prophecies-fulfilled-in-Jesus-Christ/.

CHAPTER 12

1. John 19:30 and Luke 23:46.

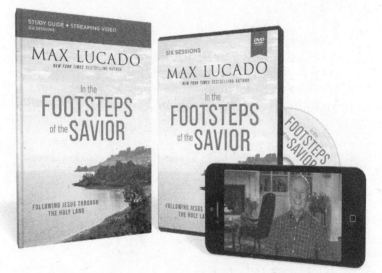

FIND FRESH STRENGTH AND PURPOSE IN THE POWER OF THE HOLY SPIRIT

WWW.MAXLUCADO.COM

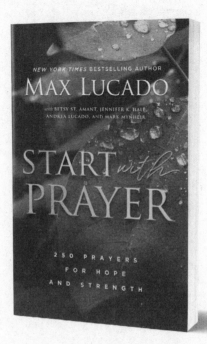

Start with Prayer is a special collection of 250 topically arranged prayers, designed to help you find the strength and hope you need before you try to solve the problem on your own. It is the perfect go-to when you want to pray but lack the words to do so.

WWW.MAXLUCADO.COM

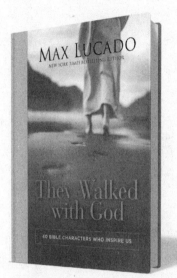

They Walked with God takes a closer look at forty of the most inspirational characters in the Bible and shares a powerful message: if God can find a place for each character in the Bible, he's carved out a spot for you too.

WWW.MAXLUCADO.COM

STUDY THE BIBLE WITH
MAX LUCADO

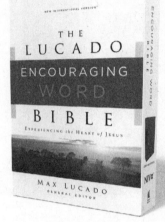

EXPAND YOUR UNDERSTANDING OF SCRIPTURE AND BE ENCOURAGED ON YOUR SPIRITUAL JOURNEY

Available in NIV and NKJV translations

WWW.MAXLUCADO.COM

Inspired by what you just read?

Connect with Max.

Hope. Pure and simple.

Listen to Max's teaching ministry, UpWords, on the radio and online. Visit www.MaxLucado.com to get FREE resources for spiritual growth and encouragement, including:

- Archives of *UpWords*, Max's daily radio program, and a list of radio stations where it airs
- Devotionals and emails from Max
- First look at book excerpts
- Downloads of audio, video, and printed material
- Mobile content

You will also find an online store and special offers.

www.MaxLucado.com

1-800-822-9673

UpWords Ministries
P.O. Box 692170
San Antonio, TX 78269-2170

Join the Max Lucado community:
Facebook.com/MaxLucado
Instagram.com/MaxLucado
Twitter.com/MaxLucado

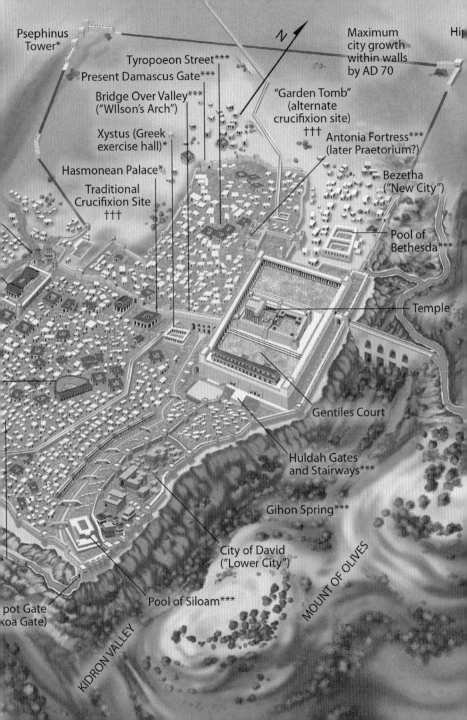

Psephinus Tower*

Tyropoeon Street***

Present Damascus Gate***

Bridge Over Valley*** ("Wilson's Arch")

Xystus (Greek exercise hall)*

Hasmonean Palace*

Traditional Crucifixion Site †††

Maximum city growth within walls by AD 70

Hi

N

"Garden Tomb" (alternate crucifixion site) †††

Antonia Fortress*** (later Praetorium?)

Bezetha ("New City")

Pool of Bethesda***

Temple

Gentiles Court

Huldah Gates and Stairways***

Gihon Spring***

City of David ("Lower City")

Pool of Siloam***

pot Gate koa Gate)

KIDRON VALLEY

MOUNT OF OLIVES

Mediterranean Sea

Tyre

UPPI
GALII

Mt. Meron

olemais

WESTERN
LOWER
GALILEE

Cana

Taricheae
(Dalmanutha)
(Magadan)
(Magdala)

Arbel Po

Sepphoris

Z

EASTERN
LOWER
GALILEE

Nazareth

*Mt.
Tabor*

Jabne

Nain

Endor

*Hill of
Moreh*